Microsoft Dynamics NAV 2016 Financial Management

Second Edition

Master the world of financial management with Microsoft Dynamics NAV 2016

Anju Bala
Cristina Nicolàs Lorente
Laura Nicolàs Lorente

BIRMINGHAM - MUMBAI

Microsoft Dynamics NAV 2016 Financial Management

Second Edition

First published: October 2013

Second edition: January 2017

Production reference: 1301216

Published by Packt Publishing Ltd.
Livery Place
35 Livery Street
Birmingham
B3 2PB, UK.
ISBN 978-1-78646-949-6

www.packtpub.com

Credits

Authors

Anju Bala
Cristina Nicolàs Lorente
Laura Nicolàs Lorente

Copy Editors

Pranjali Chury
Laxmi Subramanian

Reviewer

Stefano Demiliani

Project Coordinator

Vaidehi Sawant

Commissioning Editor

Aaron Lazar

Proofreader

Safis Editing

Acquisition Editor

Chaitanya Nair

Indexer

Tejal Daruwale Soni

Content Development Editor

Rohit Singh

Graphics

Jason Monteiro

Technical Editors

Vibhuti Gawde
Pratish Shetty

Production Coordinator

Melwyn Dsa

About the Authors

Anju Bala is MCT/MCP/MCTS in Microsoft Dynamics NAV and AX. She is an ITIL Expert and Prince 2 certified as well. She has both business and technical skills and has been working with Dynamics NAV since 2010. She started in the ERP world as a trainer, but soon evolved the skill set of a complete Dynamics NAV professional, including all the tasks involved in Dynamics NAV implementation: consulting, analysis, development, implementation, training, and support to end users. Over the course of her Dynamics NAV career, Anju has often been designated as the primary person responsible for the success and failure of a Dynamics NAV implementation. Her extensive career in the Dynamics NAV business is evidence of her success rate and expertise. She specializes in Microsoft Dynamics NAV and Microsoft Dynamics AX. You can find out more about her and get in touch with her through her LinkedIn profile at `https://in.linkedin.com/in/balaanju`.

Cristina Nicolàs Lorente has been working with Dynamics NAV since 2005. She started in the ERP world as a developer, but soon evolved into a complete Dynamics NAV professional, doing all the tasks involved in Dynamics NAV implementation: consultancy, analysis, development, implementation, training, and support to end users.

When Cristina started developing solutions for Dynamics NAV she had no idea about accounting or any kind of business workflows. They don't teach those topics for a technical university career. Soon, she discovered that it is important to know the set of tools used, but even more important to understand the meaning of whatever you develop. Without knowing accounting rules, practices, and legal requirements, it is impossible to develop useful accounting functionalities even if you are the best developer. Only when you fully understand a company's processes, will you be able to do the appropriate developments. Having that in mind, she has taken courses in accounting, warehouse management, and operations management. She is also willing to take courses on any other company-related topics.

She thinks that the best way to learn is to teach what you are learning to someone else. She has actually learned almost everything she knows about Dynamics NAV by responding to user questions on Internet forums, by writing a blog about Dynamics NAV, and of course by writing the book you have in your hands. When you have to write about something, you have to experiment, try, investigate, and read. It is definitely the best way to learn. Cristina is also a coauthor of the book *Implementing Microsoft Dynamics NAV 2013*, which had really good comments coming from different Dynamics NAV experts.

I would like to thank Isabel, who has supported me on this project. She has always believed in me and has been pushing me to find the time invested in this book. Without her, this project would have been much more difficult than it turned out to be. I would also like to thank Laura, my sister and colleague, the coauthor of this book, for always being positive about what you can reach with effort, discipline, and confidence in your own capabilities. She is the one who encouraged me to write this book. A special thanks to Josep and Josep Maria; they have given me an opportunity to professionally evolve. They have always believed in me and have given me the needed confidence to take my own steps and responsibilities. The final thanks go to all my colleagues and customers and also to all the people who helped me learn by posting questions on the forums. You have all contributed to the professional that I am today.

Laura Nicolàs Lorente started working with Dynamics NAV back in 2005, first in the support department, mostly solving functional issues and doubts. She soon jumped to full deployment: consulting, analysis, development, implementation, migration, training, and support. Right at the beginning, she realized that it was very important for a Dynamics NAV consultant to have a deep knowledge of business workflows. Technical skills are just not enough. So she started training herself in accounting, taxation, supply chain, logistics, and so on. She discovered a whole new world and found it very interesting. After having enough consultancy experience, she got to manage the first project on her own. And then, she realized that even tech and business knowledge is not enough; she also needed management skills. So, after reading different management books and trying different approaches on the projects she worked on, she decided to deepen her knowledge by taking a master's degree in project management. She is now transitioning to agile management and agile development for better project success. She continues her training in the three areas (tech, business workflows, and management) whenever she gets a chance to. The Web is a huge source of inspiration for her: groups, forums, blogs, books, and so on. She also contributes by sharing her knowledge and experience with the Spanish Dynamics NAV community. Laura is also a coauthor of the book *Implementing Microsoft Dynamics NAV 2013*, which had really good comments coming from different Dynamics NAV experts.

I would like to dedicate this book to Roc and Quim, my twin sons, who were born while writing this book. Being a mum has changed me and my life, and I am really happy with it. A new life starts from now on. I hope I will be able to teach them the values I learned from my parents, which made me be the person I am. I also want to dedicate this book to Rosa, my wife, who gave birth to such beautiful babies. She is the pillar onto which I hold and the person that gives me the energy I need to keep going. I would like to thank Cristina. She is my sister, friend, and colleague. We both wrote this book and had a great time together while writing and learning. I wish us many successful projects together--now and in the future. I'd also like to thank my family, friends, colleagues, managers, and customers who helped me grow. And special recognition to my forum and blog followers for their comments. It is nice to know that you are helping people and that they thank you for that.

About the Reviewer

Stefano Demiliani is a MCSD, MCAD, MCTS on Microsoft Dynamics NAV, MCTS on Sharepoint, MCTS on SQL Server, and a long-time expert on other Microsoft-related technologies. He has a master's degree in computer engineering from Politecnico of Turin. He works as a senior project manager and solution developer for EID (http://www.eid.it), a company in the Navlab group (http://www.navlab.it), one of the biggest Microsoft Dynamics groups in Italy, where he's also the Chief Technical Officer. He has a good amount of experience in Microsoft Dynamics NAV (from the first versions of the ERP). His main activity is architecturing and developing enterprise solutions based on the entire stack of Microsoft technologies (Microsoft Dynamics NAV, Microsoft Sharepoint, Azure, and .NET applications in general, and OLAP and BI solutions for data analysis), and he's often focused on engineering-distributed, service-based applications. Stefano works as a full-time NAV consultant (with over 15 years of international NAV projects) and he is available for architecturing solutions based on Microsoft's ERP and for NAV database tuning and optimization (performance and locking management). He's the author of different Microsoft Certified NAV add-ons (for example, the first cost accounting add-on on NAV). He has written many articles and blogs on different Microsoft-related topics and he's frequently involved in consulting and teaching. He has worked with Packt Publishing in the past on many books related to Microsoft Dynamics NAV. You can find out more about him and get in touch with him through his site http://www.demiliani.com or via Twitter (@demiliani) or Linkedin.

www.PacktPub.com

For support files and downloads related to your book, please visit www.PacktPub.com.

Did you know that Packt offers eBook versions of every book published, with PDF and ePub files available? You can upgrade to the eBook version at www.PacktPub.com and as a print book customer, you are entitled to a discount on the eBook copy. Get in touch with us at service@packtpub.com for more details.

At www.PacktPub.com, you can also read a collection of free technical articles, sign up for a range of free newsletters and receive exclusive discounts and offers on Packt books and eBooks.

https://www.packtpub.com/mapt

Get the most in-demand software skills with Mapt. Mapt gives you full access to all Packt books and video courses, as well as industry-leading tools to help you plan your personal development and advance your career.

Why subscribe?

- Fully searchable across every book published by Packt
- Copy and paste, print, and bookmark content
- On demand and accessible via a web browser

Customer Feedback

Thank you for purchasing this Packt book. We take our commitment to improving our content and products to meet your needs seriously--that's why your feedback is so valuable. Whatever your feelings about your purchase, please consider leaving a review on this book's Amazon page. Not only will this help us, more importantly it will also help others in the community to make an informed decision about the resources that they invest in to learn.

You can also review for us on a regular basis by joining our reviewers' club. **If you're interested in joining, or would like to learn more about the benefits we offer, please contact us**: customerreviews@packtpub.com.

Table of Contents

Preface   1

Chapter 1: The Sales and Purchase Processes   7

  Introducing Microsoft Dynamics NAV   8

    Importance of Financial Management   10

    Posted data cannot be modified (or deleted)   10

    No Save button   11

  Understanding master data   12

    Customers   12

    Items   15

    Vendors, resources, and locations   17

  Pricing   17

    Defining sales prices   18

    Defining sales discounts   19

    Purchase pricing   22

  Documents   22

  Document workflows   29

    Document approval   31

  Workflows   31

    Workflow process   34

  GL account cards   35

    General Journal   37

    Audit report   38

  Summary   38

Chapter 2: Managing Payments and Banks   39

  Managing due dates   39

    Payment terms   39

    Prepayments   42

    Prepayment processing flow   44

  Using credit cards and other payment methods   51

  Posting payments   52

    Suggesting vendor payments   54

    Creating and printing checks   54

  Customer balances   55

    Which invoice has been paid?   56

Vendor balances   57
Payment registration   57
Payment reconciliation   62
Payment application rules   63
The bank data conversion service   64
   Making payments with the bank data conversion service or SEPA credit
transfer   65
   Incoming and outgoing payments in NAV   69
   Data Exchange Framework   69
Bank account currency restrictions   71
Bank reconciliation   71
Summary   73

Chapter 3: Accounting Processes   75

Posting accounting transactions   75
   Standard Journal   77
   Recurring journals   78
     Allocations   79
Reporting taxes – VAT   81
   VAT settlements   83
   VAT statements   84
Managing fixed assets   86
   Creating a fixed asset and posting its acquisition cost   87
   Revaluating fixed assets   90
   Calculating depreciation   90
   Selling or disposing of a fixed asset   93
   Canceling fixed asset entries   93
Inventory valuation   94
   Choosing a costing method   94
   Calculating item entry costs   95
     Inbound entries   95
     Outbound entries   95
   Posting an inventory valuation to the general ledger   96
   Inventory valuation report   97
Closing the accounting year   98
   Closing accounting periods   98
   Running the Close Income Statement batch process   99
   Restricting allowed posting dates   101
   Posting transactions on a closed year   102
Consolidating financial statements   102

Performing consolidation   103
    Consolidating on a single database   103
    Consolidating with different databases   104
    Consolidating with other applications   106
Reporting over a consolidated company   106
Setting it up   106
    Defining business units   107
    Translating a chart of accounts   108
Deferrals   109
Summary   111

Chapter 4: Reporting and Business Intelligence   113

Understanding dimensions   113
Defining default dimensions on master data   114
Using dimensions on documents and journals   115
Using filters and flowfilters   116
Applying filters on pages   116
Applying flowfilters on pages   118
Creating views   119
Using reports   120
Displaying charts   121
The show as chart option   122
Adding charts to the Role Center page   122
Using account schedules   123
Analysis views   125
Creating an analysis view   126
Using analysis views   127
    Analysis by dimensions   127
    Analysis views as a source of account schedules   128
Business Intelligence with Excel and PowerPivot   130
Summary   132

Chapter 5: Foretelling - Budgeting and Cash Flow Management 133

Budgets   133
Creating budgets   134
Using budgets   138
Cash flow management   138
Creating manual expenses and revenues   141
Cash flow management setup   142
Summary   144

Chapter 6: Financial Management Setup   145

Understanding posting groups   145
  Specific posting groups   146
  General posting groups   147
  Tax posting groups   149
Setting up dimensions   150
Number series   151
General setup   152
Summary   154

Chapter 7: Other Financial Functionalities   155

Currencies   155
Intercompany postings   157
Accounting implications of other areas   160
  Jobs   160
  Service   161
  Warehouse   161
  Manufacturing   161
XBRL   161
E-services and document management   162
Document exchange service   162
The OCR service   164
Simple Mail Transfer Protocol (SMTP)   165
Process   165
Summary   166

Chapter 8: Fixed Asset Setup and Transactions   167

What are fixed assets?   167
The Fixed Asset cards   168
Fixed Asset transactions   169
  Journals for fixed assets   170
  Acquiring fixed assets   170
  Purchasing fixed assets   170
  Calculating and posting depreciation   171
    Manual depreciation with the FA G/L Journal   171
    Calculating depreciation automatically   172
  Write-down and appreciation of fixed assets   175
  Fixed Asset disposals   175
    Posting the disposal through the FA G/L Journal   176
  Budget Fixed Asset transactions   177
    Demonstration – Budget for future acquisition costs   178
  Reclassifiying assets   179

Transferring assets   179
Setting up maintenance information   183
Maintenance registration and costs   185
Keeping track of service visits   185
Recording maintenance costs   186
Setting up insurance information   187
The Fixed Asset Setup page   187
Insurance types   187
Insurance card   188
Attaching assets to insurance policies   189
Linking fixed assets to insurance policies   189
Linking a fixed asset to an insurance policy through an insurance journal   190
Fixed Asset reports   191
Maintenance details report   192
Insurance coverage details report   193
Fixed Asset details report   194
FA register report   195
Microsoft announces Dynamics® 365 at WPC   195
What is Microsoft Dynamics 365?   196
Summary   197
Index   199

Preface

Dynamics NAV is an **Enterprise Resource Planning** (**ERP**) system targeted at small- and medium-sized companies. An ERP is a system, a software, which integrates internal and external management information across an entire organization. If you search the Internet, you will find plenty of documentation, web forums, and all kinds of information covering Dynamics NAV from many technical points of view, but you will find little or nothing covering Dynamics NAV from a functional point of view, meant for end users. Thousands of users from all around the world who use Dynamics NAV as their main tool for daily work complain that they cannot find information about what they need from the system. And they are right.

This book is written for them, after the experience of training many end users on each implementation we have worked on. We have found out that most users do not care about system configuration; they just want to know how the system works. They contact Dynamics NAV consultants to set up when needed. But in the little end user documentation they find, each topic starts with a full setup introduction that confuses readers and possibly even discourages them from reading.

In this book, we have changed the established structure of official manuals. Instead, we have used a logical structure that makes it easy to read and very easy to understand; this is how we teach Dynamics NAV in our training courses, and this is how people tell us they have learned and understood the application.

Don't think this book is meant only for financers and accountants; this book is also meant for Dynamics NAV consultants and developers. You need complete functional knowledge of Dynamics NAV to become an expert, and this book can help you with it.

You will never finish learning about new features and functionalities. The idea behind the book is that you learn enough to be able to keep learning on your own. Every single field in every single table can hide a mini functionality that can help you in your work.

What this book covers

Chapter 1, *The Sales and Purchase Process*, explains how these two essential business areas in all companies can be handled in Dynamics NAV. It also shows how Dynamics NAV translates all the transactions into accountancy language on the fly. In this chapter, you will learn how to create new customers and vendors, set up your pricing policies, and the documents used when selling and purchasing, as well as their workflows.

Chapter 2, *Managing Payments and Banks*, discusses how companies have to charge for the items delivered and have to pay for the services received after invoicing. In this chapter, you will learn how to manage different payment terms and methods and to analyze customer and vendor extracts and their outstanding balances.

To verify that the statements your bank provides you agree with the payments and charges you have posted into the system, you can use the Bank reconciliation feature, which is explained in the chapter.

Chapter 3, *Accounting Processes*, explains how to handle accounting tasks such as reporting taxes, fixed asset management, inventory valuation, posting payroll accrual entries, and provisions. This chapter also covers other accounting transactions, annual accounting close, and consolidation with other companies.

Chapter 4, *Reporting and Business Intelligence*, discusses the tools that can help you with the analysis, both inside and outside the application. The previous chapters teach you about data entry and data processing tasks. Once the data is introduced into the system, you should be able to analyze it.

This chapter explains how dimensions can be used to tag entries so that you can group entries with similar characteristics. This will allow you to report on the data in a way that is meaningful to the company.

Dynamics NAV has a bunch of reports that can be used out of the box. Account Schedules and Analysis view are features that allow users to create their own reports. You can also use the Business Intelligence tools included in Excel by linking it with your Dynamics NAV database.

Chapter 5, *Foretelling - Budgeting and Cash Flow Management*, explains how accounting rules are based on fait accompli, but companies need to anticipate and predict events. In Dynamics NAV, budgets are used to plan costs, revenues, and resources and can be used to set up goals and measure performance. The cash flow management functionality is meant to help companies to predict future cash needs.

Chapter 6, *Financial Management Setup*, explains that in Dynamics NAV everything leads to accounting, but most of the operations inside the Financial Management module can be carried out with little accountancy knowledge. You need to set up the system so that it can translate transactions into accountancy language according to your company's rules.

This chapter covers the general setup, the dimensions setup, the creation and configuration of posting groups, and the definition of number series.

Chapter 7, *Other Financial Functionalities*, explains briefly about currencies, intercompany postings, XBRL, and accounting implications on areas such as jobs, services, warehouse, or manufacturing. The previous chapters cover the most important aspects of financial management with Dynamics NAV. But the application has a lot more possibilities.

Chapter 8, *Fixed Asset Setup and Transactions*, explains the complete life cycle of a Fixed Asset from acquisition to disposal from the GL, AP, and FA modules. In this chapter, we will cover all the FA setups, transactions, budgeting, insurance, and maintenance entries. At the end, we will also see the major Fixed Asset reports.

What you need for this book

To successfully follow the examples in this book, you will need an installation of Microsoft Dynamics NAV 2016.

Who this book is for

This book is meant for financers and accountants that are using or going to use Dynamics NAV as their ERP and financial management system.

It is also meant for Dynamics NAV consultants and project managers that will help organizations to use the system for their daily work.

The book will also be very helpful to Dynamics NAV developers that want to understand how the standard application is used in organizations, to help them develop better features and better integrate existing ones.

Conventions

In this book, you will find a number of text styles that distinguish between different kinds of information. Here are some examples of these styles and an explanation of their meaning.

New terms and **important words** are shown in bold. Words that you see on the screen, for example, in menus or dialog boxes, appear in the text like this: "A **Search Name** can also be provided if you refer to your customer by its commercial name rather than by its fiscal name"

Warnings or important notes appear in a box like this.

Tips and tricks appear like this.

Reader feedback

Feedback from our readers is always welcome. Let us know what you think about this book-what you liked or disliked. Reader feedback is important for us as it helps us develop titles that you will really get the most out of. To send us general feedback, simply e-mail feedback@packtpub.com, and mention the book's title in the subject of your message. If there is a topic that you have expertise in and you are interested in either writing or contributing to a book, see our author guide at www.packtpub.com/authors.

Customer support

Now that you are the proud owner of a Packt book, we have a number of things to help you to get the most from your purchase.

Downloading the color images of this book

We also provide you with a PDF file that has color images of the screenshots/diagrams used in this book. The color images will help you better understand the changes in the output. You can download this file from https://www.packtpub.com/sites/default/files/down loads/MicrosoftDynamicsNAV2016FinancialManagement_ColorImages.pdf.

Errata

Although we have taken every care to ensure the accuracy of our content, mistakes do happen. If you find a mistake in one of our books-maybe a mistake in the text or the code-we would be grateful if you could report this to us. By doing so, you can save other readers from frustration and help us improve subsequent versions of this book. If you find any errata, please report them by visiting `http://www.packtpub.com/submit-errata`, selecting your book, clicking on the **Errata Submission Form** link, and entering the details of your errata. Once your errata are verified, your submission will be accepted and the errata will be uploaded to our website or added to any list of existing errata under the Errata section of that title.

To view the previously submitted errata, go to `https://www.packtpub.com/books/content/support` and enter the name of the book in the search field. The required information will appear under the **Errata** section.

Piracy

Piracy of copyrighted material on the Internet is an ongoing problem across all media. At Packt, we take the protection of our copyright and licenses very seriously. If you come across any illegal copies of our works in any form on the Internet, please provide us with the location address or website name immediately so that we can pursue a remedy.

Please contact us at `copyright@packtpub.com` with a link to the suspected pirated material.

We appreciate your help in protecting our authors and our ability to bring you valuable content.

Questions

If you have a problem with any aspect of this book, you can contact us at `questions@packtpub.com`, and we will do our best to address the problem.

1
The Sales and Purchase Processes

Sales and purchase are two essential business areas in all companies. In many organizations, the salesperson or the purchase department are the ones responsible for generating quotes and orders. People from the finance area are the ones in charge of finalizing the sales and purchase processes by issuing the documents that have an accountant reflection: invoices and credit memos.

In the past, most systems required someone to translate all the transactions to accountancy language, so they needed a financier to do the job. In Dynamics NAV, anyone can issue an invoice, with zero accounting knowledge needed. But a lot of companies keep their old division of labor between departments. This is why we have decided to explain the sales and purchase processes in this book.

This chapter explains how their workflows are managed in Dynamics NAV.

In this chapter, you will learn the following:

- What Dynamics NAV is and what it can offer to your company
- How to define the master data needed to sell and purchase
- How to set up your pricing policies
- What kind of documents you can issue
- The workflows inside the sales and purchase area

Introducing Microsoft Dynamics NAV

Dynamics NAV is an **Enterprise Resource Planning** (**ERP**) system aimed at small and medium-sized companies.

An ERP is a system, a piece of software, that integrates the internal and external management information across an entire organization. The purpose of an ERP system is to facilitate the flow of information between all business functions inside the boundaries of the organizations. An ERP system is meant to handle all the organization areas on a single software system. This way, the output of an area can be used as an input of another area.

Dynamics NAV 2016 covers the following functional areas:

- **Financial Management**: This includes accounting, G/L budgets, account schedules, financial reporting, cash management, receivables and payables, fixed assets, VAT reporting, intercompany transactions, cost accounting, consolidation, multicurrency, and intrastat
- **Sales and Marketing**: This area covers customers, order processing, pricing, contacts, and marketing campaigns
- **Purchase**: The purchase area includes vendors, order processing, approvals, planning, costing, and other such areas
- **Warehouse**: In the warehouse area, you will find inventory, shipping and receiving, locations, picking, and assembly
- **Manufacturing**: This area includes product design, capacities, planning, execution, costing, and subcontracting
- **Job**: Within the job area, you can create projects, phases and tasks, planning, time sheets, work in process, and other such areas
- **Resource Planning**: This helps you to manage resources, capacity, and so on.
- **Service**: Within this area, you can manage service items, contracts, order processing, planning and dispatching, and service tasks
- **Human Resources**: This helps you to manage employees, absences, and so on

Some of these areas will be covered in detail in this book.

Dynamics NAV offers much more than robust financial and business management functionalities. It is also a perfect platform to customize the solution to truly fit your company's needs. If you have studied different ERP solutions, by now you would know that customizations to fit your specific needs will always be necessary. Dynamics NAV has a reputation as being easy to customize, which is a distinct advantage.

Since you will probably have customizations in your system, you might find some differences with what is explained in this book. Your customizations could imply the following:

- You have more functionality in your implementation
- Some steps are automated, so some manual work can be avoided
- Some features behave different from what they explained here
- There are new functional areas in your Dynamics NAV

In addition, Dynamics NAV has around forty different country localizations that are meant to cover country-specific legal requirements or common practices.

Many people and companies have already developed solutions on top of Dynamics NAV to cover horizontal or industry-specific needs, and they have registered their solution as an add-on, such as the following:

- Solutions for the retail industry or the food and beverages industry
- **Electronic Data Interchange (EDI)**
- Quality or maintenance management
- Integration with third-party applications such as electronic shops, data warehouse solutions, or CRM systems

These are just a few examples. You can find almost 2,000 registered third-party solutions that cover all kinds of functional areas. If you feel that Dynamics NAV does not cover your needs and you will need too much customization, the best solution will probably be to look for an existing add-on and implement it along with your Dynamics NAV.

Anyway, with or without an add-on, we said that you will probably need customizations. How many customizations can you expect? This is hard to tell as each case is particular, but we'll try to give you some highlights.

If your ERP system covers 100 percent of your needs without any customization, you should worry. This means that your procedures are so standard that there is no difference between you and your competence. You are not offering any special service to your customer, so they are only going to measure you by the price they are getting.

On the other hand, if your Dynamics NAV only covers a low percentage of your needs, it could just mean two things: this is not the product you need, or your organization is too chaotic and you should re-think your processes to standardize them a bit.

Some people agree that the ideal scenario would be to get about 70-80 percent of your needs covered out of the box, and about 20-30 percent as customizations to cover those needs that make you different from your competitors.

Importance of Financial Management

In order to use Dynamics NAV, all organizations have to use the Financial Management area. It is the epicenter of the whole application. Any other area is optional and their usage depends on the organization's needs. The sales and the purchase areas are also used in almost any Dynamics NAV implementation.

Actually, accountancy is the epicenter, and the general ledger is included inside the Financial Management area. In Dynamics NAV, everything leads to accounting. It makes sense as accountancy is the act of recording, classifying, and summarizing, in terms of money, the transactions and events that take place in the company.

Every time the warehouse guy ships an item, or the payment department orders a transfer, these actions can be written in terms of money using accounts, credit, and debit amounts.

An accountant could collect all the company transactions and translate them one by one to the accounting language. But this means manual duplicate work, a lot of chances of getting errors and inconsistencies, and no real-time data.

On the other hand, Dynamics NAV is capable of interpreting such transactions and translating them to accountancy on the fly. In Dynamics NAV, everything leads to accountancy, so all the company's employees are helping the financial department with their job. The financers can now focus on analyzing the data and taking decisions, and they don't have to bother on entering the data anymore.

Posted data cannot be modified (or deleted)

One of the first things you will face when working with Dynamics NAV is the inability to modify what has been posted, whether it's a sales invoice, a shipment document, a general ledger entry, or any other data. Any posted document or entry is unchangeable.

This might cause frustration, especially if you are used to working with other systems that allow you to modify data. However, this feature is a great advantage since it ensures data integrity. You will never find an unbalanced transaction.

If you need to correct any data, the Dynamics NAV approach is to post new entries to null the incorrect ones, and then post the good entries again. For instance, if you have posted an invoice, and the prices were wrong, you will have to post a credit memo to null the original invoice and then issue a new invoice with the correct prices:

Document No.	Amount	
Invoice 01	1000	
Credit Memo 01	-1000	This nulls the original invoice
Invoice 02	800	

As you can see, this method that is used for correcting mistakes always leaves a track of what was wrong and how we solved it. Users get the feeling that they have to perform too many steps to correct the data with the addition that everyone can see that there was a mistake at some point. Our experience tells us that users tend to pay more attention before they post anything in Dynamics NAV, which leads to making fewer mistakes in the first place.

So another great advantage of using Dynamics NAV as your ERP system is that the whole organization tends to improve their internal procedures, so no mistakes.

No Save button

Dynamics NAV does not have any kind of **Save** button anywhere in the application. Data is saved into the database while it is being introduced. When you enter data in one field, right after you leave the field, the data is already saved. There is no undo feature.

The major advantage is that you can create any card (for instance, **customer card**), any document (for instance, **sales order**), or any other kind of data without knowing all the information that is needed.

Imagine you need to create a new customer. You have all their fiscal data except their VAT number. You could create the card, fill in all the information except the VAT Registration No. field, and leave the card without losing the rest of the information. When you have figured out the VAT number of your customer, you can come back and fill it in. The not-losing-the-rest-of-the-information part is important.

Imagine that there actually was a **Save** button; you spend a few minutes filling in all the information and, at the end, click on **Save**. At that moment, the system carries out some checks and finds out that one field is missing. It throws you a message saying that the customer card cannot be saved. So you basically have two options:

- To lose the information introduced, find out the VAT number for the customer, and start all over again.
- To cheat. Fill the field with some wrong value so that the system actually lets you save the data. Of course, you can come back to the card and change the data once you've found out the right one. But nothing will prevent any other user posting a transaction with the customer in the meantime.

Understanding master data

Master data is all the key information to the operation of a business. Third-party companies, such as customers and vendors, are part of the master data. The items a company manufactures or sells are also part of the master data.

Many other things can be considered master data, such as the warehouses or locations, the resources, or the employees.

The first thing you have to do when you start using Dynamics NAV is loading your master data into the system. Later on, you will keep growing your master data by adding new customers, for instance. To do so, you need to know what kind of information you need to provide.

Customers

We will open a customer card to see what kind of information is stored in Dynamics NAV about customers. To open a customer card, follow these steps:

1. Navigate to `Departments/Sales & Marketing/Sales/Customers`.
2. You will see a list of customers, find No. `10000 The Cannon Group PLC`.
3. Double-click on it to open its card, or select it and click on the **View** icon found on the **Home** tab of the ribbon.

The following screenshot shows the customer card for **The Cannon Group PLC**:

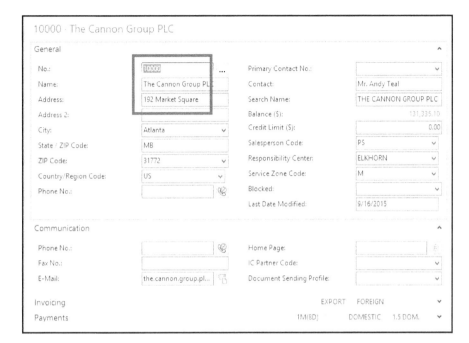

Customers are always referred to by their **No.**, which is a code that identifies them. We can also provide the following information:

- Name, address, and contact: A **Search Name** can also be provided if you refer to your customer by its commercial name rather than by its fiscal name.
- Invoicing information: It includes posting groups, price and discount rates, and so on.
- You may still not know what a posting group is, since it is the first time these words are mentioned on this book. At this moment, we can only tell you that posting groups are important. But it's not time to go through them yet. We will talk about posting groups in `Chapter 6`, *Financial Management Setup*.
- Payments information: It includes when and how we will receive payments from the customer.
- Shipping information: It explains how to ship items to the customer.

Besides the information you see on the card, there is much other information we can introduce about customers. Take a look at the **Navigate** tab found on the ribbon:

The other information that can be entered is as follows:

- **Information about bank accounts**: This is so that we know where we can request the payments. Multiple bank accounts can be set up for each customer
- **Credit card information**: This is in case customers pay using this procedure.
- **Prepayment information**: This is in case you require your customers to pay in advance, either totally or partially
- **Additional addresses**: This is where goods can be shipped (**Ship-to Addresses**).
- **Contacts**: You may relate to different departments or individuals from your customers
- **Relations**: This is the relation between our items and the customer's items (cross references)
- **Prices and discounts**: This will be discussed in the *Pricing* section

But customers, just as any other master data record, do not only have information that users inform manually. They have a bunch of other information that is filled in automatically by the system as actions are performed:

- **History**: You can see it on the right side of the card and it holds information such as how many quotes or orders are currently being processed or how many invoices and credit memos have been issued.
- **Entries**: You can access the ledger entries of a customer through the **Navigate** tab. They hold the details of every single monetary transaction done (invoices, credit memos, payments, and so on).
- **Statistics**: You can see them on the right side and they hold monetary information such as the amount in orders or the amount of goods or services that have been shipped but not yet invoiced.
- **Balance**: This is a sum of all invoices issued to the customer minus all payments received from the customer.

Not all the information we have seen on the customer card is mandatory. Actually, the only information that is required if you want to create a transaction is to give it a **No.** (its identification) and to fill in the posting group's fields (**Gen. Bus. Posting Group** and **Customer Posting Group**). All other information can be understood as default information and setup that will be used in transactions so that you don't have to write it down every single time. You don't want to write the customer's address in every single order or invoice, do you?

Items

Now, let's take a look at an item card to see what kind of information is stored in Dynamics NAV about items. To open an item card, follow these steps:

1. Navigate to `Departments/Sales & Marketing/Inventory & Pricing/Items`.
2. You will see a list of items. Find item `1000 Bicycle`.
3. Double-click on it to open its card.

The following screenshot shows the item card for item `1000 Bicycle`:

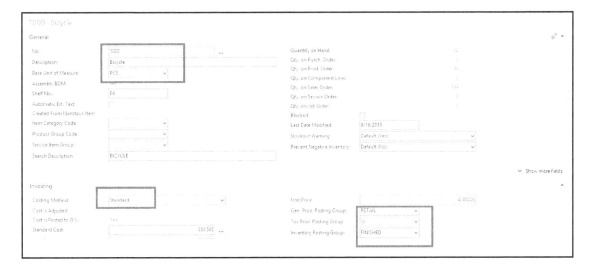

As you can see in the screenshot, items first have a **No.**, which is a code that identifies them. For an item, we can enter the following information:

- **Description**: This is the item's description. A **Search Description** can also be provided if you better identify an item using a different name.
- **Base unit of measure**: This is the unit of measure in which most quantities and other information such as **Unit Price** for the item will be expressed. We will see later what other units of measure can be used as well, but the Base is the most important one and should be the smallest measure in which the item can be referred.
- **Classification**: The **Item Category Code** and **Product Group Code** fields offer a hierarchical classification to group items. The classification can fill in the invoicing information we will see in the next point.
- **Invoicing information**: This includes posting groups, the costing method used for the item, and so on. Posting groups are explained in Chapter 6, *Financial Management Setup*, and costing methods are explained in Chapter 3, *Accounting Processes*.
- **Pricing information**: This is the item's unit price and other pricing configuration that we will cover in more detail in the *Pricing* section.
- **Foreign trade information**: This is needed if you have to do Instrastat reporting.
- **Replenishment, planning, item tracking, and warehouse information**: These fast-tabs are not explained in detail because they are out of the scope of this book. They are used to determine how to store the stock and how to replenish it.

Besides the information you see on the item card, there is much other information we can introduce about items through the **Navigate** tab found on the ribbon:

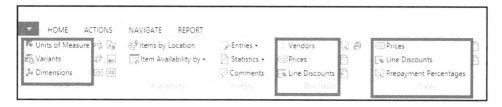

As you can see, the other information that can be entered is as follows:

- **Units of measure**: This is useful when you can sell your item either in units, boxes, or other units of measure at the same time.
- **Variants**: This is useful when you have multiple items that are actually the same one (thus, they share most of the information) but with some slight differences. You can use variants to differentiate colors, sizes, or any other small difference you can think of.
- **Extended texts**: This is useful when you need long descriptions or technical info to be shown on documents.
- **Translations**: This is used so that you can show the item's descriptions in other languages, depending on the language used by your customers.
- **Prices and discounts**: This will be discussed in the *Pricing* section.

As with customers, not all the information in the item card is mandatory.

Vendors, resources, and locations

We will start with third-parties–customers and vendors. They work exactly the same way. We will just look at customers, but everything we will explain about them can be applied to vendors as well. Then, we will look at items, and finally, we will take a brief look at locations and resources.

The concepts learned can be used in resources and locations, and also to other master data such as G/L accounts, fixed assets, employees, service items, and so on.

Pricing

Pricing is the combination of prices for items and resources and the discounts that can be applied to individual document lines or to the whole document.

Prices can be defined for items and resources and can be assigned to customers. Discounts can be defined for items and documents and can also be assigned to customers.

Both prices and discounts can be defined at different levels and can cover multiple pricing policies. The following diagram illustrates different pricing policies that can be established in Dynamics NAV:

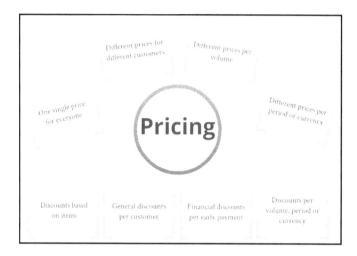

Defining sales prices

Sales prices can be defined in different levels to target different pricing policies.

The easiest scenario is when we have a single price per item or resource. That is, the **One single price for everyone** policy. In that case, the sales price can be specified on the item card or on the resource card, in a field called **Unit Price**.

In a more complex scenario, where prices depend on different conditions, we will have to define the possible combinations and the resulting price.

We will explain how prices can be configured for items. Prices for resources can be defined in a similar way, although they offer fewer possibilities.

To define sales prices for an item, follow these steps:

1. Navigate to `Departments/Sales & Marketing/Inventory & Pricing/Items`.
2. You will see a list of items. Find item `1936-S BERLIN Guest Chair, yellow`.
3. Double-click on it to open its card.
4. On the **Navigate** tab, click on the **Prices** icon found under the **Sales** group.
5. The **Edit – Sales Prices** page will open:

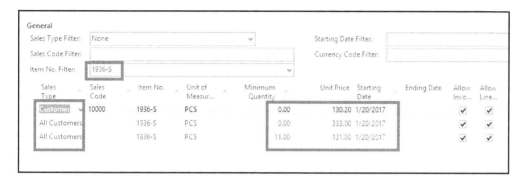

As you can see in the screenshot, multiple prices have been defined for the same item. A specific price will only be used when all the conditions are met. For example, a `Unit Price` will be used for any customer that buys item `1936-S` after `20/01/2017` but only if they buy a minimum of `11` units.

Different fields can be used to address each of the pricing policies:

- A combination of the **Sales Type** and **Sales Code** fields enable the different prices for different customer policies
- The **Unit of Measure Code** and **Minimum Quantity** fields are used on the different prices per volume policy
- The **Starting Date**, **Ending Date**, and **Currency Code** fields are used on the different prices per period or currency policy

They can all be used at the same time to enable mixed policies.

When multiple pricing conditions are met, the price that is used is the one that is most favorable to the customer (the cheapest one).
Imagine `Customer 10000` belongs to the `RETAIL` price group. On `20/01/2017` he buys 20 units of item `1936-S`. There are three different prices that could be used: the one defined for him, the one defined for its price group, and the one defined to all customers when they buy at least `11` units. Among the three prices, `130.20` is the cheapest one, so this is the one that will be used.

The prices can be defined including or excluding VAT.

Defining sales discounts

Sales discounts can be defined in different levels to target different pricing policies.

We can also define item discounts based on conditions. This addresses the **Discounts based on items** policy and also the **Discounts per volume, period or currency** policy, depending on which fields are used to establish the conditions.

In the following screenshot, we can see some examples of item discounts based on conditions, which are called **Line Discounts** because they will be applied to individual document lines:

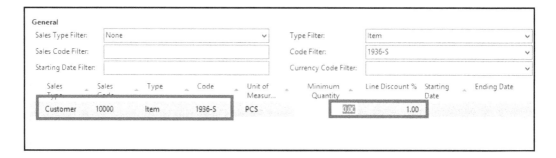

 In some cases, items or customers may already have a very low profit for the company and we may want to prevent the usage of line discounts, even if the conditions are met.

A field called **Allow Line Disc** can be found on the customer card and on sales prices. By unchecking it, we will prevent line discounts being applied to a certain customer or when a specific sales price is used.

Besides the line discounts, invoice discounts can be defined to use the **General discounts per customer** policy. Invoice discounts apply to the whole document and they depend only on the customer.

Follow these steps to see and define invoice discounts for a specific customer:

1. Open the customer card for customer 10000, The Cannon Group PLC.
2. On the **Navigate** tab, click on **Invoice Discounts**.

The following screenshot shows that customer `10000` has an invoice discount of **5** percent:

 Just like line discounts, invoice discounts can also be disabled using a field called **Allow Invoice disc.** that can be found on the item card and on sales prices.

There is a third kind of discount, payment discount, which can be defined to use the **Financial discounts per early payments** policy. This kind of discount applies to the whole document and depends on when the payment is done. Payment discounts are bound to a **Payment Term** and are to be applied if the payment is received within a specific number of days.

The following screenshot shows the payment terms that can be found by navigating to `Departments/Sales & Marketing/Administration/Payment Terms`:

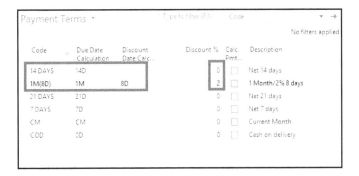

As you can see, a **2%** payment discount has been established when the **1M(8D)** Payment Term is used and the payment is received within the first eight days.

Purchase pricing

Purchase prices and discounts can also be defined in Dynamics NAV. The way they are defined is exactly the same as you can define sales prices and discounts. There are some slight differences:

- When defining single purchase pricing on the item card, instead of using the **Unit Price** field, we will use the **Last Direct Cost** field. This field gets automatically updated as purchase invoices are posted.
- Purchase prices and discounts can only be defined per single vendor and not per group of vendors as we could do in sales prices and discounts.
- Purchase discounts can only be defined per single item and not per group of items as we could do in sales discounts.
- We cannot prevent purchase discounts being applied.
- Purchase prices can only be defined excluding VAT.

Documents

Dynamics NAV is not an accountancy system, but an Enterprise Management system. Invoices are not the general ledger entries that resume them, but the document that you ship to your customer. The ledger entries are just a result of posting the document.

Documents are used to create transactions bound to one customer (or vendor) and to one or many items or resources.

Let's see how documents work by creating a sales invoice. There are other types of document. They will be explained in the next section.

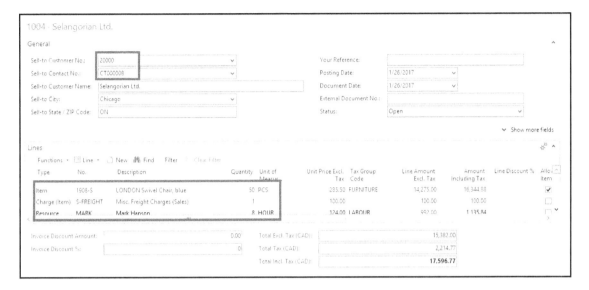

To create an invoice such as the one in the previous screenshot, perform the following steps:

1. Navigate to `Sales & Marketing/Order Processing/Sales Invoices`.
2. Click on the **New** button found on the ribbon bar.
3. A new blank invoice opens.

 You will get a definitive number for the invoice once you post it.

4. On the **Sell-to Customer No.** field, start typing the code 20. As you type, a drop-down list shows all the results that match the **No.** typed so far:

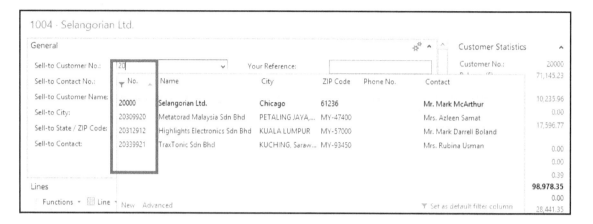

TIP

You can change the default field used as a filter. To do so, check the heading of the column you want to set as default. The little funnel icon will move to the new column. Now, click on the **Set as default filter column** option.

5. A message will tell us that the customer has an overdue balance and will ask us for confirmation to proceed. Click on **Yes**.

6. On the **Line** tab, create lines by filling in the fields of the following table:

Type	No.	Quantity	Unit Price Excl. VAT
Item	1908-S	50	
Charge (Item)	S-FREIGHT	1	100
Resource	MARK	8	
G/L Account	6610	1	15

Let's explain the different types of lines that can be used:

- **Item**: This is used when you need to sell an inventory item. When the invoice is posted, it will create an item entry to reduce its stock.
- **Charge (Item)**: This is used to adjust the costs of items. In our example, the freight charges will count as sales amount for the items, and therefore it might adjust the benefit of this particular sale. Charges can be used either on the sales and purchase area, on the same document, or in a different document. You have charged you customer for the freight; your carrier will charge you. When you get your vendor's invoice, you will need to use charges to adjust the cost of the sale.
- **Resource**: It can be employees, machinery, or other company resources.
- **G/L accounts**: Yes, you can also use G/L accounts in documents. In an ideal scenario, you will try to avoid them for two reasons: you need accounting knowledge to select the correct account, and you cannot define prices and other commercial info.
- **Fixed asset**: This is used to buy or sell fixed assets.

A blank type is used for comments. You can enter text in the **Description** field.

Item charges require one extra step to be performed before the invoice is ready to post.

7. Select the freight charge line, and click on the **Line** icon and then choose the **Item Charge Assignment** option. Write 1 in the **Qty. to Assign** field and close the page.

The **Get Shipment Lines** and **Get Return Receipt Lines** processes are used to select lines from other documents to be charged.

8. To get an overview of the invoice before it is posted, use the **Statistics** option found on the ribbon bar. You can also press *F7* to access this option:

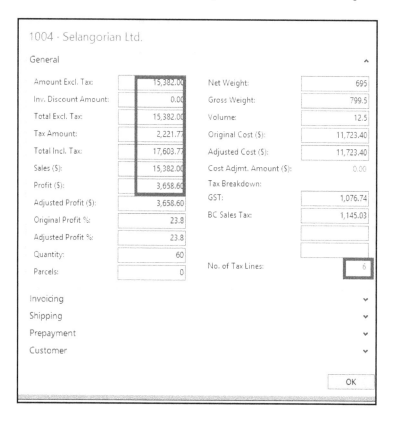

In this page, you can change both the fields shown in the previous screenshot.

9. Go back to the invoice. Choose **Post** from the ribbon bar or press *F9*.

10. The invoice is already posted. It has been moved from the `Sales Invoices` list to the `Posted Sales Invoice` list. You can access it by writing `Posted Documents/Posted Sales Invoices` on the navigation bar.

The posted invoice has created multiple entries on different areas of the application. Let's see them:

- **General ledger entries**: The system has translated the invoice to accounting language. We selected the customer, so it knew what account from group 23 to use. We sold an Item, so the system knew what income account to use, and so on. Dynamics NAV is capable to choose the right accounts, thanks to some setup tables called **Posting groups**. They are covered in detail in `Chapter 6`, *Other Financial Functionalities*:

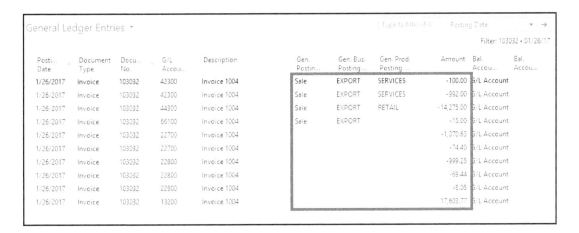

Posti... Date	Document Type	Docu... No.	G/L Accou...	Description	Gen. Postin...	Gen. Bus. Posting ...	Gen. Prod. Posting ...	Amount	Bal. Accou...	Bal. Accou...
1/26/2017	Invoice	103032	42300	Invoice 1004	Sale	EXPORT	SERVICES	-100.00	G/L Account	
1/26/2017	Invoice	103032	42300	Invoice 1004	Sale	EXPORT	SERVICES	-992.00	G/L Account	
1/26/2017	Invoice	103032	44300	Invoice 1004	Sale	EXPORT	RETAIL	-14,275.00	G/L Account	
1/26/2017	Invoice	103032	66100	Invoice 1004	Sale	EXPORT		-15.00	G/L Account	
1/26/2017	Invoice	103032	22700	Invoice 1004				-1,070.63	G/L Account	
1/26/2017	Invoice	103032	22700	Invoice 1004				-74.40	G/L Account	
1/26/2017	Invoice	103032	22800	Invoice 1004				-999.25	G/L Account	
1/26/2017	Invoice	103032	22800	Invoice 1004				-69.44	G/L Account	
1/26/2017	Invoice	103032	22800	Invoice 1004				-8.05	G/L Account	
1/26/2017	Invoice	103032	13200	Invoice 1004				17,603.77	G/L Account	

For this book, we used a demonstration company called **CRONUS Canada Inc.**, that uses the British chart of accounts. You can use the general chart of accounts of your country, or you can define a customized one.

- **TAX entries**: They are created when invoices are posted. They will be used later on to post the VAT Settlement and to report VAT to the authorities:

Entry No.	Posting Date	Docum... No.	Document Type	GST/HST	Type	Base	Amount	Tax Calculatio...	Bill-to/Pay No.
41	1/26/2017	103032	Invoice		Sale	-115.00	0.00	Sales Tax	20000
42	1/26/2017	103032	Invoice		Sale	-14,275.00	-1,070.63	Sales Tax	20000
43	1/26/2017	103032	Invoice		Sale	-992.00	-74.40	Sales Tax	20000
44	1/26/2017	103032	Invoice		Sale	-14,275.00	-999.25	Sales Tax	20000
45	1/26/2017	103032	Invoice		Sale	-992.00	-69.44	Sales Tax	20000
46	1/26/2017	103032	Invoice		Sale	-115.00	-8.05	Sales Tax	20000

- **Customer ledger entries**: They are used to keep track of all the transactions posted to one customer. Customer ledger entries are also used to manage receivables. The **Remaining Amount** field tells us how much money the customer owes us for this invoice. It will be zero when the invoice is completely paid:

Posting Date	Docum... Type	Docu... No.	Cust... No.	Description	Currency Code	Original Amount	Amount	Remaining Amount	Due Date
1/26/2017	Invoice	103032	20000	Invoice 1004		17,603.77	17,603.77	17,603.77	2/9/2017

- **Item ledger entries**: Since we sold 50 units, we need to decrease the item stock. Item ledger entries help us keep track of the company stock. It also keeps track of the **Sales Amount** and **Cost Amount** of this particular entry:

Posti... Date	Entry Type	Document Type	Document No.	Item No.	Quantity	Invoiced Quantity	Remaining Quantity	Sales Amount (Actual)	Cost Amount (Actual)	Cost Amount (Non-Invtbl.)	Open
1/26/2017	Sale	Sales Ship...	102043	1908-S	-50	-50	-50	14,375.00	-11,125.00	0.00	✓

- **Value entries**: The **Sales Amount** and **Cost Amount** shown in each **Item Ledger Entry** are the sum of their value entries. In future, the cost of this particular item entry might change if we post new item charges or the item gets revaluated. If any of this happens, new value entries will be created:

Posting Date	Item Ledger E...	Entry Type	Adj...	Document Type	Docu... No.	Item Charge No.	Description	Sales Amount (Actual)	Cost Amount (Expected)	Cost Amount (Actual)	Item Ledger Entry Quantity	Valued Quantity
1/26/2017	Sale	Direct Cost	☐	Sales Invoice	103032			14,275.00	0.00	-11,125.00	-50	-50
1/26/2017	Sale	Direct Cost	☐	Sales Invoice	103032	S-FREIGHT	Misc. Freight Charges (Sales)	100.00	0.00	0.00	0	-50

The values entered will be used later on to know the changes in inventory in a period and post it in the general ledger entry.

- **Resource ledger entries**: The resource called MARK worked 8 hours to assemble the item we sold. We keep track of the resource, thanks to their ledger entries. We also know the cost and total price for each entry:

Posti... Date	Entry Type	Docu... No.	Resource No.	Description	Quantity	Unit of Measur...	Total Cost	Total Price	Cha...	Entry No.
1/26/2017	Sale	103032	MARK	Mark Hanson	-8	HOUR	-598.40	-992.00	✓	55

As you can see, one single invoice has generated 18 different entries in different ledgers. A financer will mainly focus on general ledger and VAT entries, while the warehouse guy will focus on item ledger entries, and the resource manager will focus on resource entries. One single invoice impacts on all areas of the company. So we have demonstrated what was told in the introduction: *An ERP system is meant to handle all the organization areas on a single software system. This way, the output of an area can be used as input of another area.*

Document workflows

In the previous section, we have seen what a document is. In this section, we will see how many documents exist in Dynamics NAV, how they are related to each other, and which are the commonly used workflows to create them. We will see sales documents, but the exact same purchase documents exist in Dynamics NAV.

There are two kinds of document in Dynamics NAV:

- **Open documents**: They hold the information that we will use to start an action or a transaction. An order, for instance, is the beginning of the action of shipping items to our customers. Open documents can be modified.
- **Posted documents**: They hold the result of a transaction that has been posted. They can be understood as historical documents and they cannot be modified. A shipment, for instance, is the result of shipping items to our customers.

The following diagram shows the available documents that exist in Dynamics NAV. There are other warehouse-specific documents that could be used on the sales and purchase processes, but we have skipped them because they are out of the scope of this book:

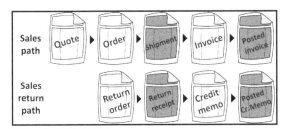

Documents in white are open documents, while those in grey are posted documents.

Not all documents have to be used. Some can be skipped and some may appear multiple times. For example, you could not use **Quote**, **Order**, **Shipment**, **Return order**, and **Return receipt**, and thus only use **Invoice**, **Posted invoice**, **Credit memo**, and **Posted Cr.Memo**. You can also use **Order**, which may lead to multiple **Shipments** (when the order is shipped partially) and then use a single **Invoice** to group all shipments and end up having a single **Posted Invoice**. This scenario is shown in the following diagram:

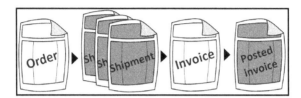

Actually, in an invoice, we can group multiple shipments, no matter if they are shipments from the same order or from different orders. There is still another possible workflow, not using invoices and generating the posted invoice from the order:

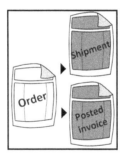

There are many other possible combinations, since all the workflows we have seen could start with a quote document, for instance. We have not seen different workflows for the sales return path, but the same workflows can be used.

Document approval

Dynamics NAV has a document approval functionality that can be applied over open documents to prevent users from posting them (and thus reaching the next document, a posted document) while they have not been approved.

Document approval can be set up in different ways so that not all documents have to go through an approval process. Only the documents that met certain conditions will actually require someone to approve them. We can decide the following:

- Which kinds of open document will require approval.
- The hierarchy of approvers. The hierarchy is based on the maximum amount each approver can approve.
- The conditions that should be met to require approval for a specific document. All the possible conditions are based on the document amounts.

Workflows

A workflow enables you to design and execute business processes within the application system. A simple workflow is the pairing of a single **Event** and a **Response**. For the workflow, we need to perform the following setup:

- **Set up workflow users:** This is used to specify the users' number in a process sequence to receive notification:

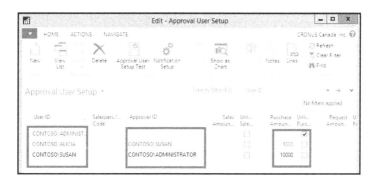

Here is the **Purchase Approver** window:

- **Set up workflow notifications:** This is used to specify when and how the notification will be generated:

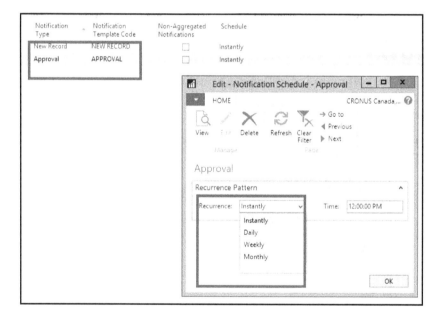

- **Set up SMTP e-mail:** This is used to send an e-mail saying we have to configure the SMTP server:

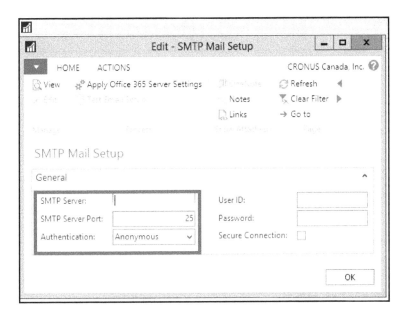

- **Workflow template**: Workflow templates are non-editable workflows that exist in Dynamics NAV:

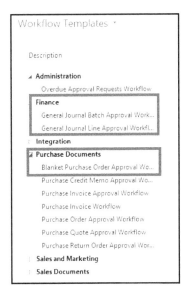

- **Create workflows**: You can create workflows that connect with your business process, such as automatic posting, that can be included as steps in workflows, preceded or followed by user tasks. Requesting and granting approval to create new records are typical workflow steps:

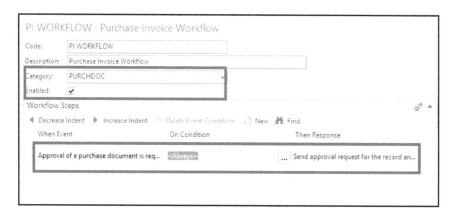

Workflow process

The following is the setup required for the workflow configuration in NAV 2016:

- Setting up approval users (including setting up a user in Windows and in Microsoft Dynamics NAV):
    - Create a user in active directory
    - Create a user in NAV and link with Windows directory
    - Set up Approval
    - Set up a workflow user group
- Setting up notifications for approval users:
    - Create a notification schedule
    - Create a notification setup
- Modifying and enabling an approval workflow:
    - View the workflow template
    - Create a new workflow

- Starting the job queue that dispatches notifications:
  - Job queue setup
- Requesting approval of a purchase order, as user A:
  - Create purchase order, after login from user A
  - Send the request to approve
- Receiving a notification and then approving the request, as user B:
  - Login from user B and approve the purchase order

GL account cards

A G/L account is used to record all the financial transactions in Dynamics NAV. An account is a unique record for each type of asset, liability, revenue, and expense.

Now, let's take a look at a G/L card to see what kind of information is stored in Dynamics NAV. To open a G/L card, follow these steps:

1. Navigate to `Departments/Financial Management/General Ledger/Chart of Account`.
2. You will see a list of G/L accounts. Find `11600 Bank Operations Cash`.
3. Double-click on it to open its card.

The following screenshot shows the G/L account card for `11600 Bank Operation Cash Account`:

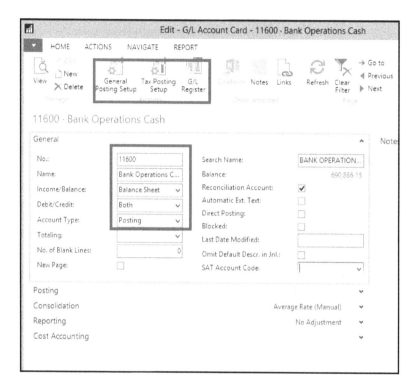

The chart of accounts window displays all the accounts, and the G/L account card window has a card for each line in the chart of accounts, so you can work with only one account at a time.

G/L accounts are always referred to by their **No.**, which is a code that identifies them. We can also provide the following information:

- The **General** tab: This is used for information about G/L account number, name, and account type (balance sheet of income account)
- The **Posting** tab: This is used for information about the general posting group and tax posting group
- The **Consolidation** tab: This is used for information about the consolidation debit or credit account and the translation method
- The **Cost Accounting** tab: This is used to show with which cost account G/L is linked

The G/L card window includes the following actions on the ribbon:

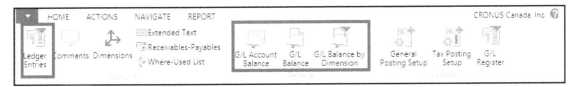

General Journal

General journals are used to post to general ledger accounts and other accounts such as bank, customer, vendor, and fixed asset accounts. Posting with a general journal always creates entries on general ledger accounts.

The following are the types of journal entries:

- **General Journal**: This is used to post simple expense and revenue transactions.
- **Standard Journal**: This is used to save the transaction that you might need to reuse again. Standard journals are used for time saving.
- **Recurring Journal**: This is used for periodic or recurring transaction for expenses and revenue.
- **Reversing Journal**: This is used to cancel or reverse the wrong posted transaction.

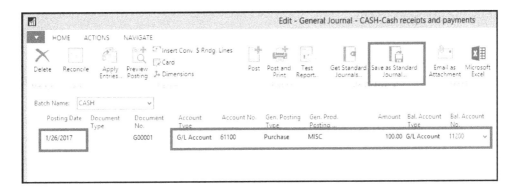

Follow these steps to enter and post in the **General Journal**:

1. Go to **General Journal** (Departments/Financial Management/General Ledger/General Journal).
2. Enter the **Posting Date**.
3. Select the G/L account as **Account Type** and select **61100** (advertising) account.
4. Enter 100 in the **Amount** field.
5. And then select cash account as offset account.
6. Post the **General Journal**.

Audit report

Navigate to Departments/Financial Management/General Ledger/ History/G/L Register.

Summary

In this chapter, we have learned that Dynamics NAV as an ERP system meant to handle all the organization areas on a single software system.

The sales and purchase processes can be held by anyone without the need of having accountancy knowledge, because the system is capable of translating all the transactions to accountant language on the fly.

Customers, vendors, and items are the master data of these areas. Its information is used in documents to post transactions. There are multiple options to define your pricing policy: from one single price to different prices and discounts per groups of customers, per volume, or per period, or currency. You can also define financial discounts per early payment.

In the next chapter, we will learn how to manage cash by showing how to handle receivables, payables, and bank accounts.

2
Managing Payments and Banks

The sales and purchase cycle does not finish after the goods are shipped, or the services are provided, and the invoice has been issued. After that, the company has to charge for items delivered and has to pay for services received.

The management of advanced payments, cash payments, or deferred payments is of vital importance for the company. In this chapter, we will learn how to do the following:

- Manage different payment methods such as payment registrations
- Handle incoming and outgoing payments in NAV
- Import bank reconciliation

Managing due dates

When you start working with a new customer or vendor, you reach an agreement with them on when are invoices due. On the **Payments** tab of the customer and vendor card, you select the **Payment Term** tab that suits the agreement. After that, the program will automatically calculate the due date when you create an invoice.

Payment terms

The **Payment Terms** page contains one line for each set of **Payment Terms** the company uses. You can create as many payment terms as you need.

Every set of payment terms must contain a **Due Date Calculation** formula that the program uses together with the document date of the invoice to calculate the due date. In addition, you can also specify a **Discount Date Calculation** formula and a **Discount %** that will be used to calculate discounts on the basis of early payments.

Navigate to `Departments/Financial Management/Receivables/Setup` to see the full list, which is shown in the following screenshot:

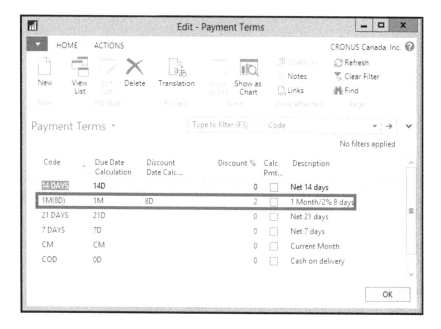

The payment term code is assigned to each customer by filling in a field called **Payment Terms Code**. When a customer uses an invoice, the payment term is copied to it and the due date gets calculated based on the document date of the invoice.

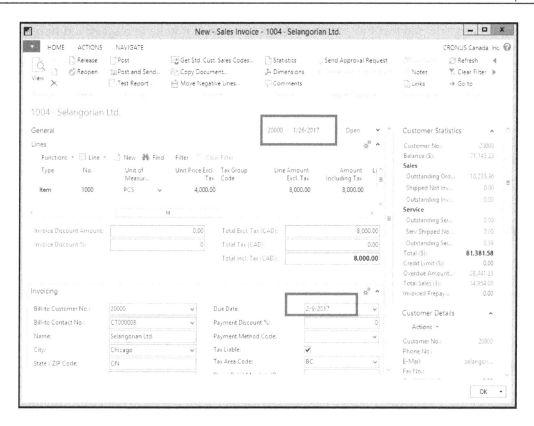

When the invoice is posted, a customer ledger entry is created with its corresponding **Due Date**. You can see the flow of data in the following diagram:

You can change the payment term in a particular invoice if you have reached a different agreement with the customer for this sale. You can also change the due date on the ledger entry if needed. At the end of the process, the system checks for due dates of ledger entries to claim charges from customers and to propose payments to vendors.

The **On Hold** field in the **Customer Ledger Entries** tab is used to indicate that the invoice should wait for approval before the payment can be reclaimed or interest added to it. You can fill the field with your initials or any other code. The same field can be found for vendor ledger entry, to indicate that an invoice cannot be paid yet. Actually, everything explained in this section also applies to vendors.

Prepayments

Prepayments are payments that are invoiced and posted to a sales or purchase prepayment order before final invoicing. As per the company and item specification, you may require to make the payment before you ship items to a customer or receive goods from a vendor.

You use the prepayments functionality in Microsoft Dynamics NAV to invoice and collect deposits that are required from customers or remit deposits to vendors.

Until the final invoice has been issued, we do not have a ledger entry to base the payments on. Prepayments can be set up for customers or vendors, regardless of the items or services included in the document. You can also specify different prepayments rates for certain items. Use a 100% rate if you need to pay it all in advance.

The following are some types of prepayments:

- **Customer and vendor prepayments**: You can specify a prepayment percent on the customer or vendor card in a field called **Prepayment %**, which will apply to all orders. Leave the field blank if you want to use prepayments for individual items.

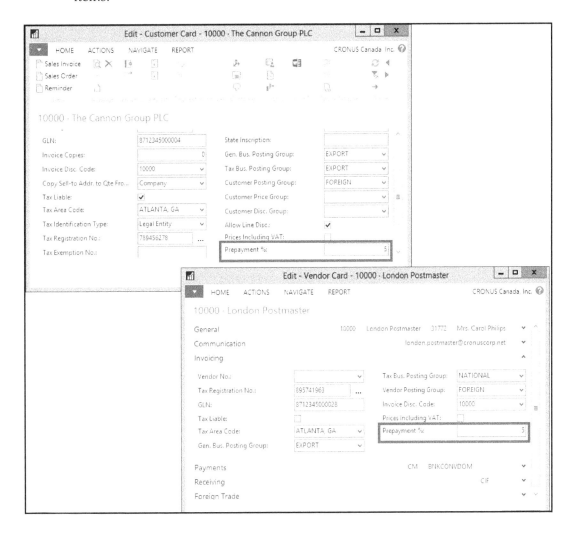

- **Item prepayments**: Similar to how you set up prices, you can specify prepayment rates for items. You can do it on the **Sales Prepayment Percentages** and **Purchase Prepayment Percentages** pages, which can be accessed from the ribbon bar of the customer and vendor list, respectively. You can also access both from the item list.

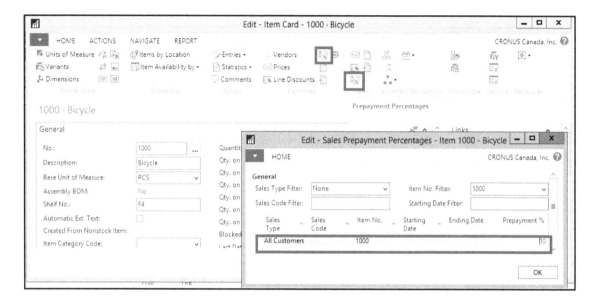

Prepayment processing flow

The steps involved in the flow of prepayment processing are as follows:

- **Set up prepayments:** First of all, we will perform the following prerequisite setups to process the prepayment in NAV 2016

- **General posting setup:** In this form, we will define the G/L account card for the **Purchase Prepayment** and **Sales Prepayment** accounts with respect to the **Gen. Business Posting** and **Gen. Product Posting** groups:

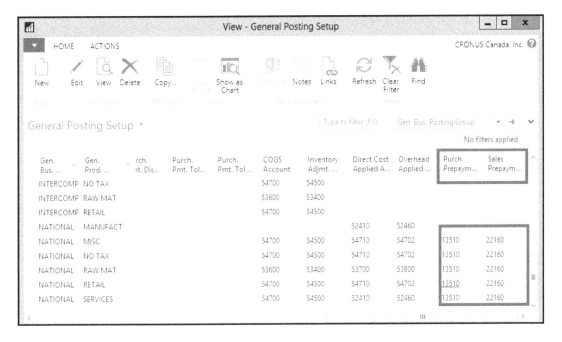

- **General ledger setup:** In this form, we will enable and disable general prepayment features:
    - Disable **Prepayment Unrealized Tax**

- **Sales & receivables setup**: In this form, we will enable and disable sales-related prepayment features:
  - Enable **Check Prepmnt. when Posting**
  - Set up a number series for prepayment documents

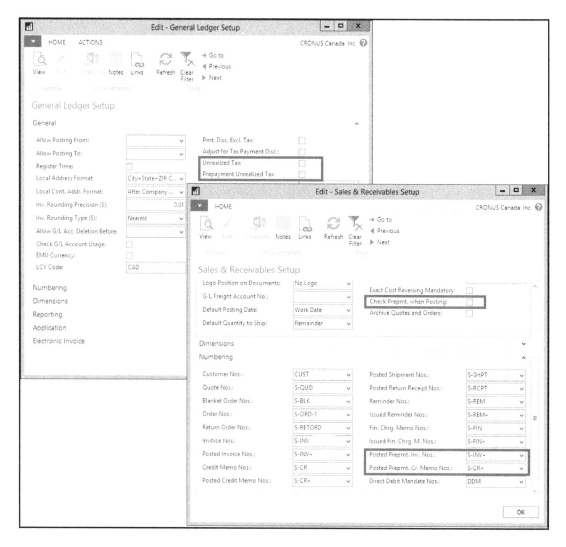

- **Assign prepayment percentage**: You can define a prepayment percentage by any of the following combinations:
  - Customer card
  - Vendor card

- Item card (customer-item)
- Item card (vendor-item)

	Specific Items	All Items
Customer	✓	✓
Customer Price Group	✓	
All Customers	✓	
Vendors	✓	✓

- **Process**: Once you have done all the preceding prepayment setups, we can move on to prepayment posting, as follows:
    1. Create a sales order with a prepayment requirement.

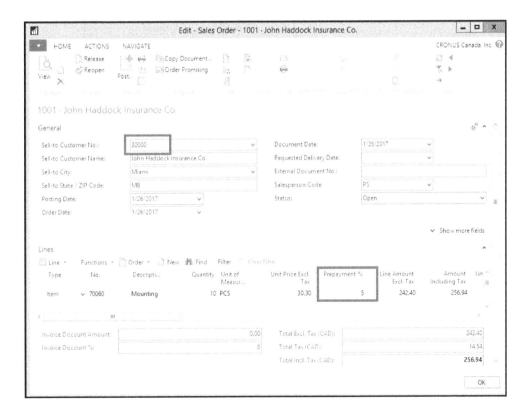

2. Send a prepayment invoice for the prepayment amount to the customer.

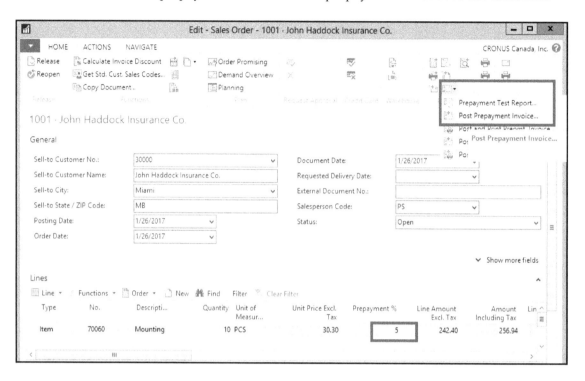

3. The customer pays the prepayment amount.

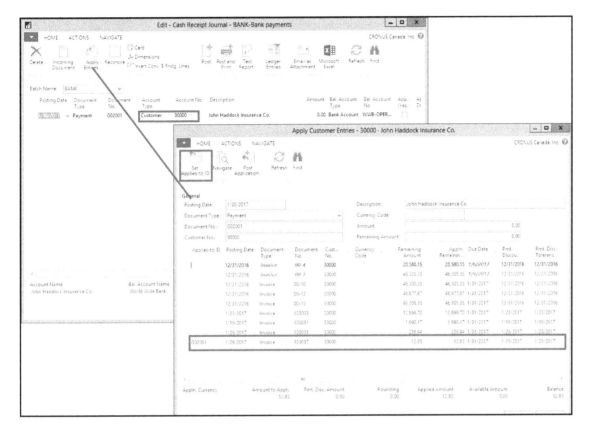

4. Apply the prepayment amount to **Sales Order**.

5. Ship and invoice the order to the customer.

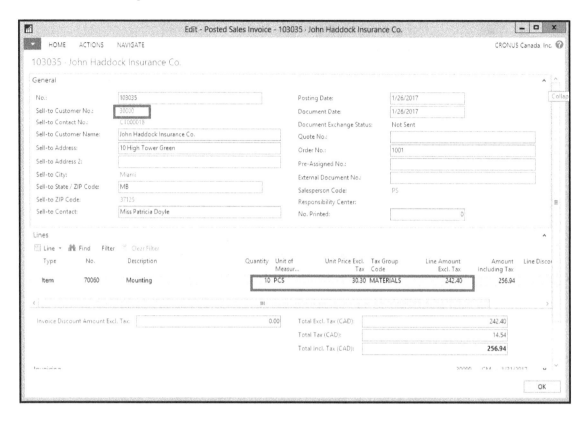

6. Verify the sales invoice for the total amount of sales order minus the prepayment amount.

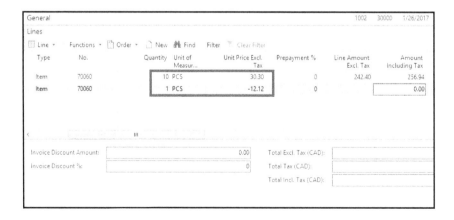

7. Receive the remaining payment from the customer and post the payment to **Sales Order**.

Using credit cards and other payment methods

Different payment methods, used both by customers and vendors, can be defined at `Departments/Financial Management/Receivables/Setup/Payment Methods`.

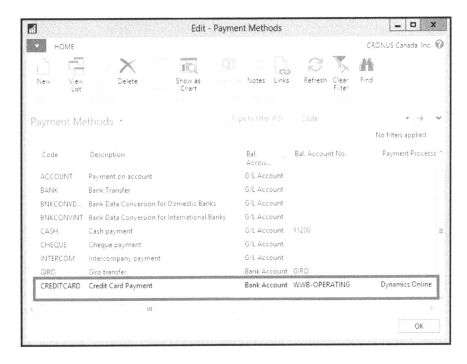

Note that both **CASH** and **CREDITCARD** have a **Bal. Account No.** defined. When you post an invoice with one of the payment methods selected, the system will create and post the payment against the invoice, so you don't have to manually do it later on. This is useful when the payment is done at the same time the invoice is raised.

When you use the credit card payment method in a sales order or invoice, you have to specify which credit card will be used. Credit cards are created on the customer card, through the **Credit Cards – Credit Cards** action found on the ribbon. Information commonly required for credit cards has to be filled in, such as the card type, the holder's name, the card number, and the expiry date. Once the credit card is selected, an authorization against the total invoice amount is required. This can either occur manually or automatically. When the invoice is posted, the actual payment is sent to the payment service. The payment is then captured and posted in Dynamics NAV. If it cannot be processed, an error message is displayed. In this case, the invoice is posted anyway, but the payment is not posted. It can be captured and posted later on using the **Cash Receipt Journal** window.

Posting payments

When you pay or are being paid, you need to register the transaction in your system, no matter what method you have used. To do so, you use the **Cash Receipt Journal** window or the **Payment Journal** window. Both work the same way, but the **Payment Journal** can also be used to print checks. To post a payment, you need to inform:

- The customer that is paying you
- The bank account that they used to make the payment
- The invoice that is being paid
- Consider the following example:

Imagine that customer `20000`, `Selangorian Ltd.` has paid us for invoice `103032`, which was due on `02/09/2017`. Let's follow the steps needed to post the payment:

1. Access the **Cash Receipt Journal** window from `Journals/Cash Receipt Journals`.
2. Select the **BANK** section and double-click on it.
3. Create a new line on the journal with the following information:

Posting Date	Document Type	Document No.
01/26/2017	Payment	This gets filled by a series number.

4. To indicate the customer that is paying:

Account Type	Account No.	Description
Customer	20000	This gets filled with the customer name. You can change it.

5. To indicate the bank account that the customer used to pay us:

Bal. Account Type	Bal. Account No.
Bank Account	WWB-OPERATING. This is the code that identifies the bank.

6. To indicate the invoice that is being paid:

Applies-to Doc. No.	
103032	When you click on this field, a page opens showing you all the pending entries for the customer. Select one.

7. Once you select a pending entry in the **Applies-to Doc. No.** field, the rest of the fields in the journal line get filled automatically: **Amount** and **Applies-to Doc. Type**. After completion, you will end up with something like this:

8. Post the transaction.

If you do not know which invoice is being paid, you can leave the **Applies-to Doc. No.** field blank and apply the payment to the invoice later on.

Suggesting vendor payments

The **Payment Journal** window has a nice feature called **suggest vendor payments**. This process creates the payment lines for you according to certain conditions, such as the following:

- It only includes invoices due until a date of your choice
- You can specify a maximum available amount for payments, so it will only suggest payments up to that amount
- You can prioritize vendors when you have a specific available amount so that the most important vendors are always paid first
- It will not process invoices that are on hold

However, this process only suggests, which means that you can modify whatever is needed before actually posting the payments.

Creating and printing checks

On the **Payment Journal**, you can also print checks to use them as a payment method for your vendors.

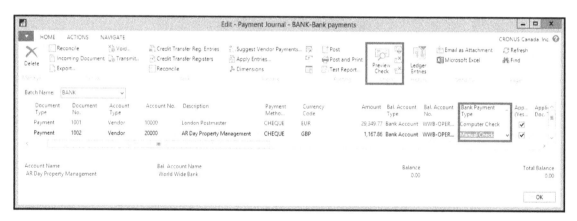

When there are one or more computer checks in your **Payment Journal**, you have to print them using the corresponding actions on the ribbon. The system will not allow you to post the payment if the checks have not been printed. However, you do not have to print anything if you have selected **Manual Check**, which means that you have created your check manually and just want Dynamics NAV to keep track of it. The posting of the journal will create check ledger entries.

Customer balances

The balance is the total amount a customer owes you or you owe to a vendor. Customer and vendor balances can be seen on their card through a field called **Balance (LCY)**. **LCY** stands for **Local Currency**. This means that, regardless of the currency used, amounts are always translated to your local currency.

To learn the details of the balance amount, you can click on the amount and the corresponding ledger entries will be shown. This can be seen in the following screenshot:

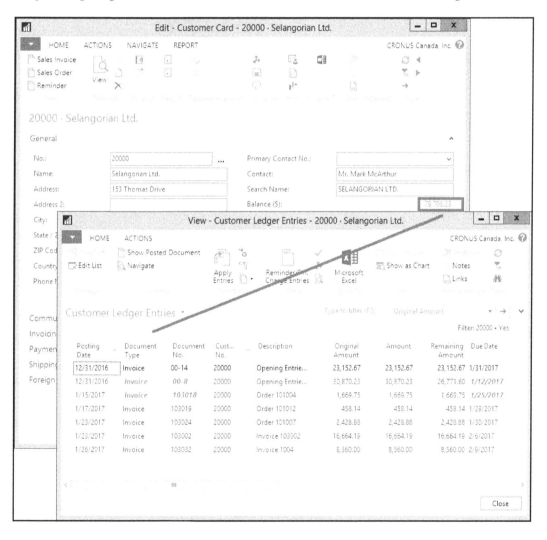

As you can see, customer `20000`, `Selangorian Ltd.` has seven pending invoices. Two of them are already due (they are shown in red) and invoice `00-8` has been partially paid (note that the remaining amount is lower than the original amount).

Which invoice has been paid?

Customer `20000`, `Selangorian Ltd.` has had many other transactions in the past. In the previous screenshot, we just viewed open transactions, but we can see them all by going back to the card and clicking on **Ledger Entries** in the **Navigate** tab.

To see which invoices are paid, compare the **Original Amount** and **Remaining Amount** columns. If the **Remaining Amount** column is zero, the full payment has been received.

Also, if the checkbox is not selected in the **Open** column, the invoice is fully settled.

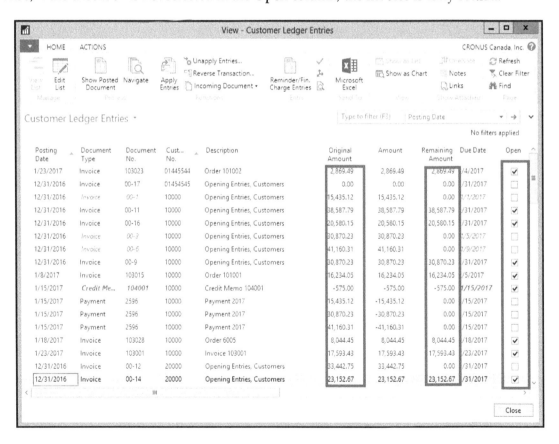

Vendor balances

There are two key fields in this page: **Remaining Amount** and **Open**. Note that many transactions are not open and show zero as the remaining amounts. This means that those invoices have already been paid or that credit memos and payments have been applied to an invoice to reduce its remaining amount:

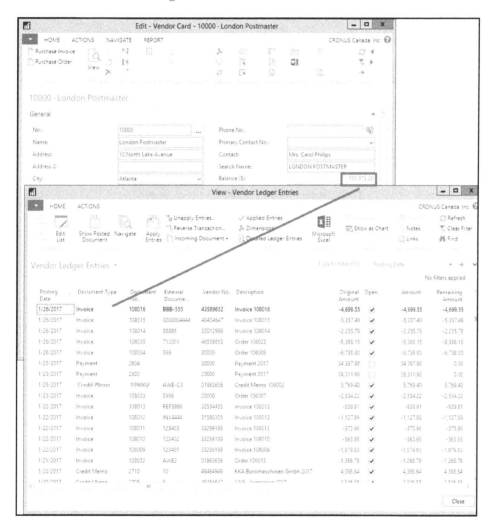

Select a ledger entry and click on **Applied Entries** in the ribbon to know how a certain transaction has been applied. You can then reapply entries.

Payment registration

The **payment registration** functionality is a unique method of handling customer receipts without creating entries through the **Cash Receipt Journal**. This functionality is designed to support users in tasks involved in balancing internal accounts, using actual cash figures to ensure effective collection from customers. To perform this, we have to perform the following steps:

1. Go to `Departments/Financial Management/Cash Management/ Payment Registration`.

2. Set up **Payment Registration**.

3. **Change Amount Received or Date Received**: The **Payment Registration** window shows all open customer ledger entries. Normally, you only have to mark the entries, post them, and then you are done.

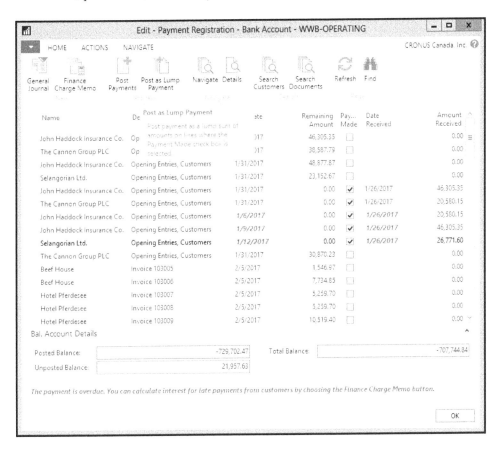

4. **Lump Payment**: This covers multiple invoices for one customer with a single payment.

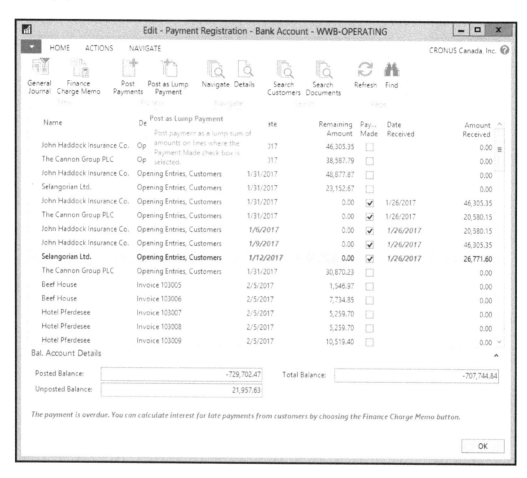

5. **Finance charge for overdue amounts:** A **Finance Charge Memo** window can be created directly from the **Payment Registration** window by selecting the **Finance Charge Memo** function.

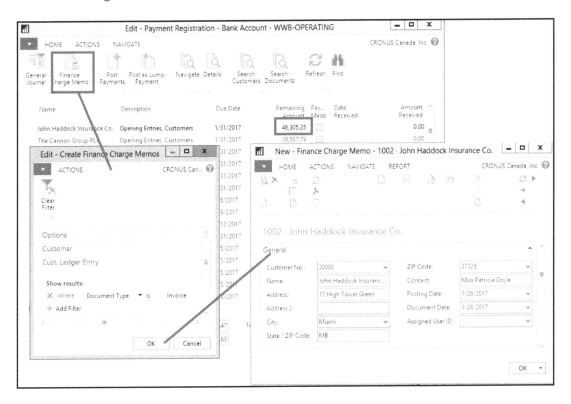

6. **Handling payment discounts**: When a payment is received within the payment discount period, the deducted amount will automatically be added and the invoice and the payment will be fully applied and closed after posting the payment.

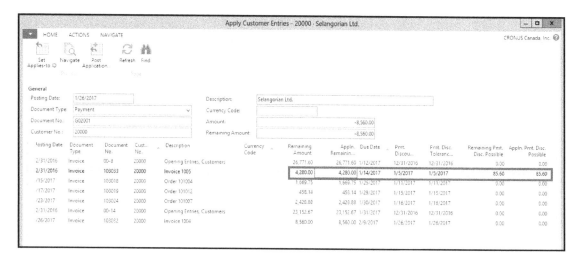

Payment reconciliation

A payment reconciliation journal is where we specify payments, either incoming from customers or outgoing to vendors, that have been recorded as transactions on your electronic bank site and that need to be applied to their related open entries.

You can perform the following main activities in the **Payment Reconciliation Journal** window:

- Import files with bank transactions for payments that have been made to or from your bank account and then automatically apply the payments to their related open entries.

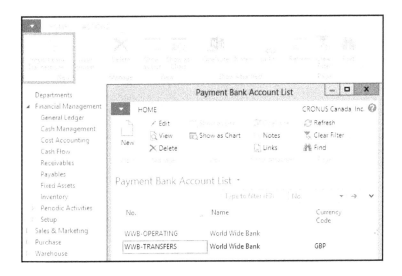

- Review and manually apply payments that were applied automatically to wrong open entries, or were not applied at all, from the **Payment Reconciliation Journal** window, shown as follows:

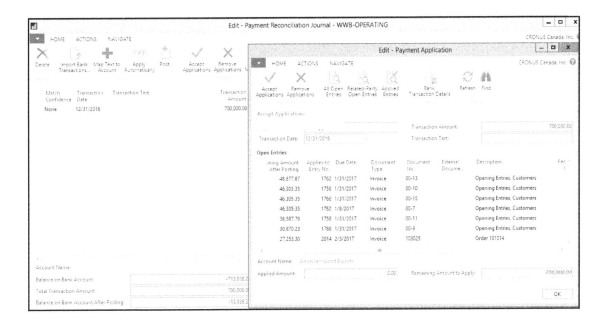

Payment application rules

In the **Payment Application Rules** window, you set up rules to govern how payments should be automatically applied to their related open entries when you use the **Apply Automatically** function in the **Payment Reconciliation Journal** window. For this, refer to the following screenshot:

Match Confidence	Priority	Related Party Matched	Doc. No./Ext. Doc. No. Matched	Amount Incl. Tolerance Matched
High	1	Fully	Yes - Multiple	One Match
High	2	Fully	Yes - Multiple	Multiple Matches
High	3	Fully	Yes	One Match
High	4	Fully	Yes	Multiple Matches

The bank data conversion service

The bank data conversion service is available out-of-the-box without additional charge to all Microsoft Dynamics NAV customers.

The bank data conversion service is used for the following:

- Enabling users to export payment files from Microsoft Dynamics NAV in any format required by their bank to enable efficient processing of outgoing payments
- Enabling users to import bank statement files from any bank in the format required by Microsoft Dynamics NAV to enable efficient reconciliation of payments and their bank accounts
- Providing support for many banks on all Microsoft localized versions of Dynamics NAV

Making payments with the bank data conversion service or SEPA credit transfer

In the **Payment Journal** window, you can process payments to your vendors by exporting a file together with the payment information from the journal lines. You can then upload the file to your electronic bank where the related money transfers are processed.

To enable SEPA credit transfers, you must first set up a bank account, a vendor, and the general journal batch that the payment journal is based on.

You then prepare payments to vendors by automatically filling in the **Payment Journal** window with due payments with specified posting dates.

- **Activate the bank data conversion service**: This is used for any bank statement file converted to a format in which you can import or export your bank data requirements:

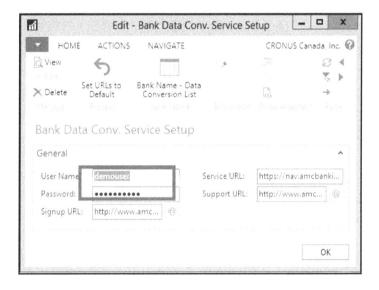

- **Payment method for vendor**: To perform a SEPA credit transfer in the payment journal, we have to specify the **Bank Data Conversion** payment method in the vendor card:

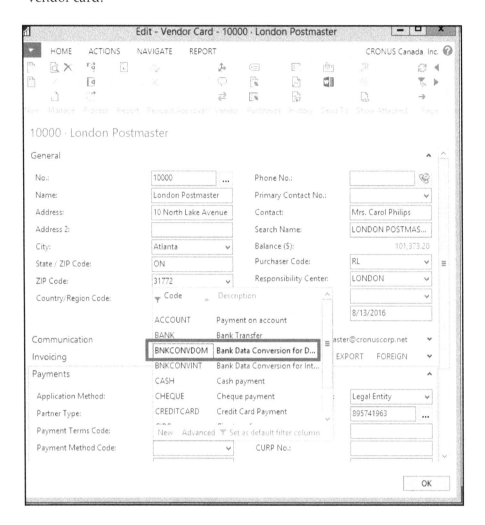

- **Bank statement import format**: We also need to link either the **Bank Data Conversion Service** or **SEPA CAMT** in the bank's card, to import the statement into Microsoft dynamics NAV 2016:

- **Suggest vendor payments**: Perform this to fill the **Payment Journal** with lines for due payments to vendors, with the posting dates based on the due date of the related purchase documents:

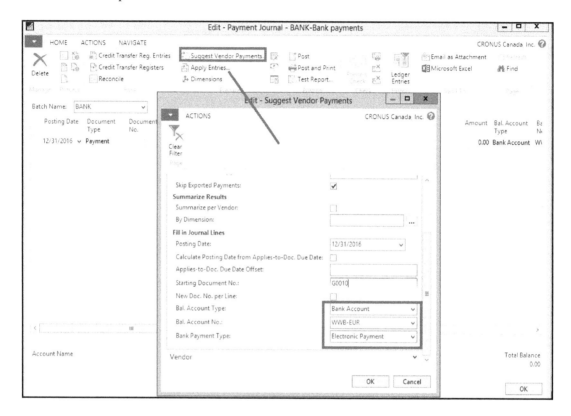

- **Export payments to a bank file**: When you are ready to make payments to your vendors using the **Payment Journal** window, you can export a file with the payment information on the journal lines. You can then upload the file to your electronic bank to process the related money transfers:

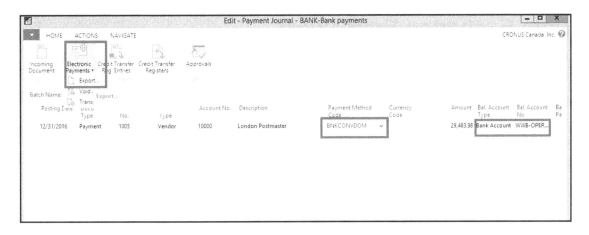

- **Post journals**: When the electronic payment is successfully processed by the bank, post the **Payments Journal** to affect the vendor, G/L, and bank account respectively.

Incoming and outgoing payments in NAV

A new feature called **Payment Reconciliation** Journal enables users to import bank transaction data into a dedicated UI and automatically open entries representing customer and vendor documents. Features include advanced record matching, strong review tools, and the possibility to freely define the payment match tolerance and to modify the generic matching algorithm.

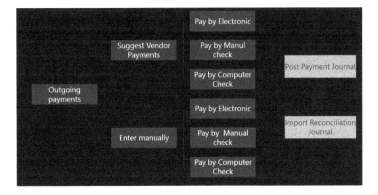

Data Exchange Framework

The **Data Exchange Framework** is used to define the format of files for exchange of data in bank files, electronic documents, currency exchange rates, and other with ERP systems; these vary depending on the provider of the data file or stream and on the country/region.

The following diagram shows the architecture of the Data Exchange Framework:

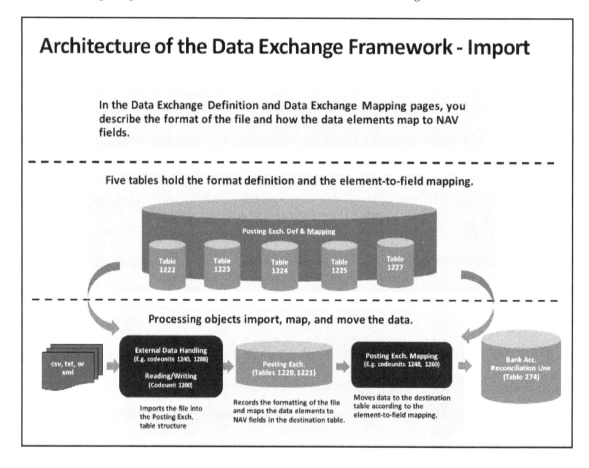

Bank account currency restrictions

After you have set up your bank accounts, you may need to transfer an amount between two bank accounts that have the same and different currency codes.

The following screenshot shows the bank account currency restriction for posting a transaction:

Bank Account Currency Code	Bank Payment Type = Computer Check or Manual Check	Bank Payment Type = Blank
Blank (LCY)	Checks are only printed for LCY payment lines. Only LCY payment lines post.	Payment lines with any currency code including LCY post.
Currency Code	Checks are only printed for payment lines with the same currency code as the bank account. Only payment lines with the same currency code as the bank account post.	Only payment lines with the same currency code as the bank account post.

Bank reconciliation

The purpose of the bank reconciliation feature is to check whether the statements your bank provides you with agree with the bank account ledger entries that you have been creating while posting payments. It helps you check whether there is any cash movement that you have not posted into the system yet. At the end of a given period, the statement ending balance must equal the balance of the bank account in Dynamics NAV.

To create a new bank account reconciliation, follow these steps:

1. Go to `Departments/Financial Management/Cash Management/Bank Account Reconciliations` and click on **New**.
2. Select the `WWB-OPERATING` code in the **Bank Account No.** field.
3. Select `03/31/2017` as the statement date and write `-600000` as the **Statement Ending Balance**.
4. Click on the **Suggest Lines…** option from the ribbon bar and click on **OK**.
5. New reconciliation lines are created as copies of open bank ledger entries.
6. Check the reconciliation lines against the bank statement lines.
7. Post the lines.

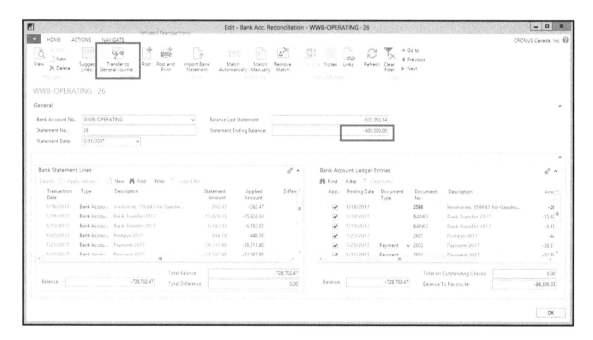

In the preceding screenshot, most of the bank statement entries have been posted in the system, but the first and the last ones are missing. You can manually create them in the bank reconciliation and use the **Transfer to General Journal…** action to transfer them to the corresponding journal, complete the transaction there, and post them.

Once the missing statement lines are posted, from the bank reconciliation page use the **Apply Entries** actions to select new bank ledger entries to be applied against the manually created bank reconciliation lines.

And finally, post the bank reconciliation using the **Post** action found on the ribbon. Once a reconciliation is posted, its ending balance will become the initial balance of the next statement.

Summary

In this chapter, you learned how to manage payments using different payment methods both for customers and vendors. We have also learned how to create and post those payments in the system and how they affect the balances for customers and vendors. Finally, we have seen how to reconcile banks ledger entries in Dynamics NAV with the actual bank statement.

In the next chapter, we will see how different accounting processes are managed.

3
Accounting Processes

So far we have seen the accounting tasks that require most of an accountant's time, because they are the bulkiest tasks: posting sales, purchases, and payments. But there are many other accounting tasks that have to be performed.

In this chapter, we will explore the following accounting processes:

- Posting accounting transactions
- Reporting taxes - VAT (Tax Posting setup)
- Managing fixed assets
- Inventory valuation
- Closing the accounting year
- Consolidating financial statements
- Deferrals

Posting accounting transactions

The system can automatically create and post many accounting transactions such as those for sales and purchase invoices, for instance. There are many other transactions that end up in an accounting entry automatically created by the system. We will actually see this in this chapter: taxes, fixed assets, inventory valuations, and so on.

You will probably need to post many other accounting transactions that are not managed by the system, such as payroll accrual entries, provisions, or others. You can post all these transactions using the **General Journal**.

The **General Journal** can be accessed by navigating to **Financial Management** | **General Ledger** and clicking on **General Journal**.

In the **General Journal**, you manually create the necessary transaction lines, indicating the **Account No.**, **Bal. Account No.**, and **Amount** as shown in the following screenshot. There are many other fields that could be filled in, actually, but we will start with an easy example:

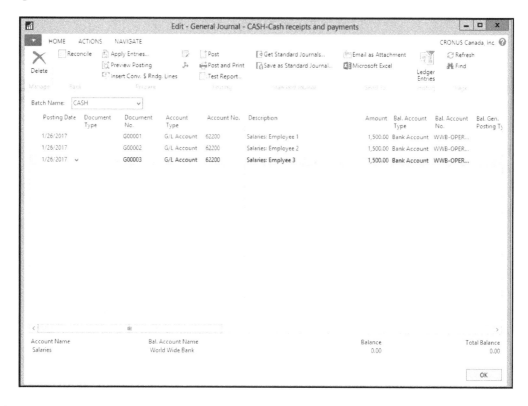

When posting this journal, the system will create six G/L entries: three on account `8720` with a debit amount, three on the account corresponding to the bank `WWB-OPERATING` with a credit amount.

Instead of indicating a balancing account on every single journal line, you can leave the **Bal. Account No.** field empty and create a fourth journal line where you will indicate the balancing account and amount, as shown in the following screenshot:

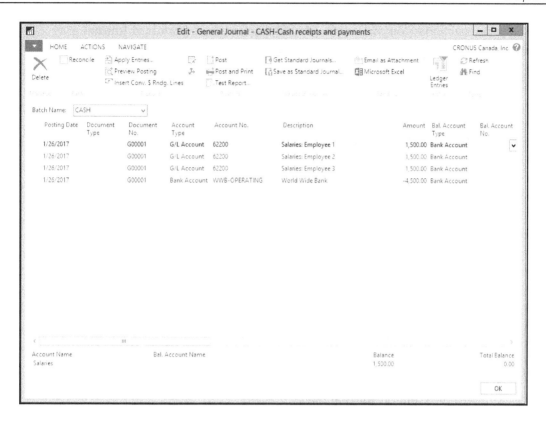

When posting this journal, the system will create four G/L entries: three on account 8720 with a debit amount, one on the account corresponding to the bank WWB-OPERATING with a credit amount.

On the **General Journal**, you can create and post all the accounting transactions you need. There is no limit. Just keep in mind that when the accounting transaction you want to post involves customers, vendors, banks, or fixed assets, you should use the appropriate **Account Type** rather than directly using the final G/L account to which the transaction has to be posted. This way, the transaction will also be reflected on the customer, vendor, bank, or fixed asset card.

Standard Journal

Transactions in a general journal are usually created manually by a user every time they have to post a new transaction. Some accounting transactions are used over and over, because they have to be posted once a week or once a month.

For those transactions, you can use the standard journals. A **Standard Journal** is a transaction template that you create and can use as many times as needed.

To create a standard journal, perform the following steps:

1. Open the **General Journal** page.
2. Create the General Journal lines you want to save as a Standard Journal.
3. Click on **Save as Standard Journal....**
4. Select **Code** and enter a **Description** for the **Standard Journal**.
5. You can choose whether you want to save the amount on the Standard Journal. Take a look at the following screenshot:

6. Click on **OK**.

To use a **Standard Journal**, perform the following steps:

1. Open the **General Journal** page.
2. Click on **Get Standard Journals....**
3. Select the appropriate **Standard Journal**.
4. Journal lines will be created on the **General Journal**.
5. Complete the General Journal lines by entering the posting date and other information you may require for the actual transaction.
6. Post the **General Journal**.

Recurring journals

Recurring journals are useful for transactions that are posted frequently with few or no changes. The journal lines are preserved after posting, so when you open them, they already contain journal lines that can be reviewed, adjusted, and posted on a recurring basis.

When using recurring journals with the reversing option, the system posts the transaction and it also posts the reversing entries on the following day. Another usage of recurring journals is to post allocations based on amounts or percentages.

You can find a recurring journal for the following journals:

- Each General Journal type (general, assets, cash receipts, payments, inter-company, jobs, sales, and purchase)
- Fixed asset journals
- Item journals
- Resource journals

You create and post recurring journal lines just like you do with standard journals. Additionally, recurring journals have the following extra fields:

Field Name	Usage
Recurring Method	This determines how the amount on the journal is treated after posting. With this field, you also determine whether the reversing entries should be posted or not.
Recurring Frequency	This contains a formula that determines how frequently an entry on the journal will be posted. For example, if the formula 1M is entered, after the journal is posted, the date is changed by adding one month. There are many other date formula possibilities. To learn more about them, check the *How to: Enter Dates and Times* topic in the Dynamics NAV **Help** menu.
Expiration Date	This is used to limit the posting period by specifying the last date that an entry can be repeated.

Allocations

Allocations are used to allocate the amount on the recurring journal line to several G/L accounts and dimensions. When you use allocations, you do not have to introduce a balancing line, as the allocation is in itself a balancing account line to the recurring journal line.

1. Navigate to **Departments | Financial Management | Fixed Assets | Periodic Activities | Recurring General Journal**.
2. To open the **Allocations** page, double-click on the **Allocated Amt.** field.

3. Allocate the amount from the original line by percentage to the different CUSTOMERGROUP dimension values, as shown in the following screenshots:

- **Fixed**: The following screenshot depicts **Fixed** (dimension value):

- **Variable**: The following screenshot depicts **Variable** (dimension value):

- **Balance**: The following screenshot depicts **Balance** (dimension value):

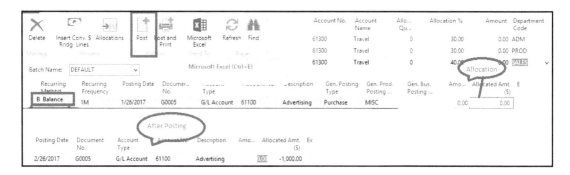

4. Close the page to go back to the recurring journal. Note that the **Allocated Amt.** field is now filled. It should match the **Amount** field but with the opposite sign.

In the example, we have allocated by percentage by filling the **Allocation** % field. The different methods to allocate amounts are as follows:

- **Allocation Quantity**: This allocates the amounts by quantities. An example is, allocating by the number of people in each department.
- **Allocation %**: This allocates the amounts by percentage.
- **Amount**: If you use one of the previous methods, the program calculates the allocated amount. You can also manually enter an allocation amount.

Reporting taxes – VAT

Value-Added Tax (**VAT**) is a tax on consumption that is paid by the end consumer. VAT is calculated on sales and purchases and reported to the tax authorities periodically.

 The general concepts of VAT are the same in all countries where VAT applies. Statement and VAT rates differ from country to country. This book is based on the Dynamics NAV worldwide (W1) database. Most Dynamics NAV country versions include localizations on VAT.

In Dynamics NAV, VAT is calculated on sales and purchases invoices and credit memos. When the documents are posted, new VAT entries are created that will be used later on to report VAT to the authorities.

VAT is calculated based on the combination of **VAT Business Posting** groups (the customer and vendor fix it) and **VAT Product Posting** groups (the items and services fix it).

In Chapter 1, *The Sales and Purchase Process*, we have posted the sales invoice number as 103023. Let's take a look at the VAT entries that were created while posting the invoice:

1. Navigate to Posted Documents/Posted Sales Invoices.
2. Locate the invoice number 103033 and click on the **Navigate** option.
3. Select the VAT Entry table, and click on the Show icon from the ribbon bar.

4. The **Tax Entries** page will show all the VAT entries created for the invoice as shown in the following figure:

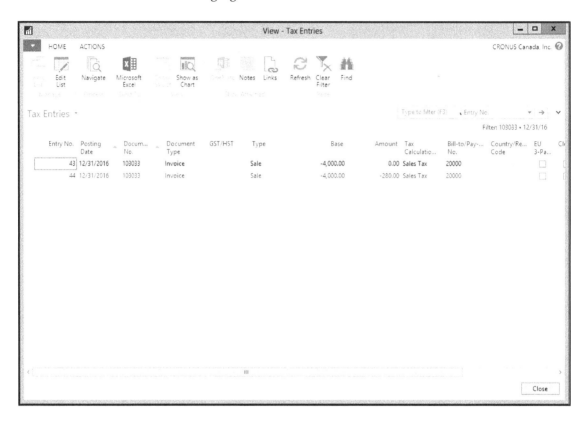

The customer fixed **NATIONAL** as **VAT Bus. Posting Group**. The invoice included an **Item**, a **Charge**, a **Resource**, and a **G/L Account**; each fixed its own **VAT Prod. Posting Group**.

Now let's see how we can calculate the VAT settlement based on these VAT entries and the rest of the VAT entries created with each invoice and credit memo.

VAT settlements

The **VAT settlement** batch job is used to calculate and post, to the **General Journal**, the net VAT amount that must be remitted to the tax authorities. Once a VAT entry has been used to post the VAT settlement amount, the system closes the entry so that you don't include it again in a new calculation.

To run the **Calc. and Post Tax Settlement** catch job, follow these steps:

1. Navigate to **Departments** | **Financial Management** | **Periodic Activities** | **VAT** | **Calc. and Post TAX Settlement**.
2. Run the report with the following options:

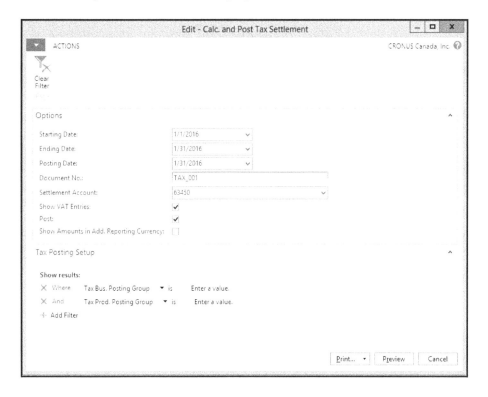

The **Starting Date** and **Ending Date** define the range of dates for the VAT entries to be settled. The **Posting Date** will be used to post the settlement amount in the general journal. For **Document No.**, type a unique number that identifies the transaction.

In the **Settlement Account** field, select the G/L Account that the net amount will be transferred to. Usually it will be a credit amount; however, if the purchase VAT amount is larger, it will be a debit amount.

Show VAT Entries
Leave it unchecked to display only the total settlement for each VAT posting group. Otherwise, all VAT entries used to calculate the settlement will be shown.

Post
Leave it unchecked to print a test report. Otherwise, the settlement amount will be posted into the general journal and the VAT entries will be closed. You will not be able to reopen them, but you will be able to run VAT statements anyway.

VAT statements

VAT statements are used to specify the basis for calculating the VAT that is payable to the tax authorities. You will usually define them once when you initially set up your company and then preview or print them periodically. To run a VAT statement, follow these steps:

1. Navigate to **Departments | Financial Management | Periodic Activities | VAT | VAT Statements**. Select the **DEFAULT** statement and double-click on it.

2. Click on the **Print…** option from the ribbon bar and run the report with the options shown in the following screenshot:

3. The VAT statement will look like this:

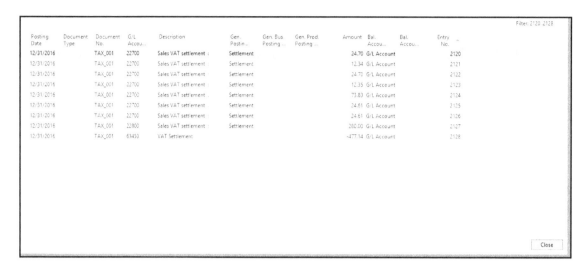

As you can see, the purpose of the VAT statement is to resume all the posted VAT entries in a manner that is useful for you, to report VAT to the authorities. VAT Statements are fully customizable and you can create as many statements as needed to match different authority formats or VAT internal reporting formats.

Managing fixed assets

Dynamics NAV provides a fully integrated fixed asset management functionality that allows you to track depreciation expenses reliably in multiple depreciation books. It is useful to have one depreciation book integrated with the general ledger, and another one for internal fixes asset calculations that do not have to be reflected in the general ledger. You can also keep track of other information relevant to fixed assets, such as maintenance cost and schedules, acquisition costs, and related insurance information.

Creating a fixed asset and posting its acquisition cost

Each fixed asset has a card, which contains all the information about the asset. To create a new one, you can follow these steps:

1. Navigate to **Departments** | **Financial Management** | **Fixed Assets** | **Fixed Assets** and click on the `New` icon from the ribbon bar.

2. A blank card opens. Press *Enter* to get a **No.** and give it a description. If the asset has a serial number, type it in the **Serial No.** field.

3. On the **Lines** Fast tab, create one line with the following information:

Field	Value
Depreciation Book Code	COMPANY
FA Posting Group	CAR
Depreciation Method	Straight-Line
Depreciation Starting Date	01/15/2016
No. of depreciation years	5

The information in this line will be used when calculating depreciation. You can create one line per **Depreciation Book** defined in the company. The **FA Posting** group specifies the accounts to which the program will post transactions involving fixed assets.

So far the **Fixed Asset Card** looks similar to the following screenshot:

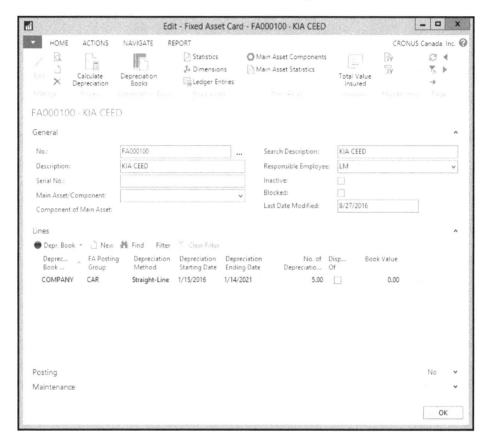

 The **Book Value** field is zero. This is because we haven't posted the acquisition cost yet. After that, the **Book Value** will decrease month on month as we depreciate the asset, and it will be zero again once completely depreciated.

To post the acquisition cost of the asset through a purchase invoice, use the following steps:

1. Create a new purchase invoice. Select the vendor, and select **1/15/2016** as **Posting Date**.
2. Create a line in the purchase invoice with the following values:

Field	Value
Type	Fixed Asset
No.	FA000100
Quantity	1
Direct Unit Cost Excl. VAT	13500

3. Post the purchase invoice.
4. Go back to the fixed asset card and note that **Book Value** is now 13500. Refer to the following screenshot:

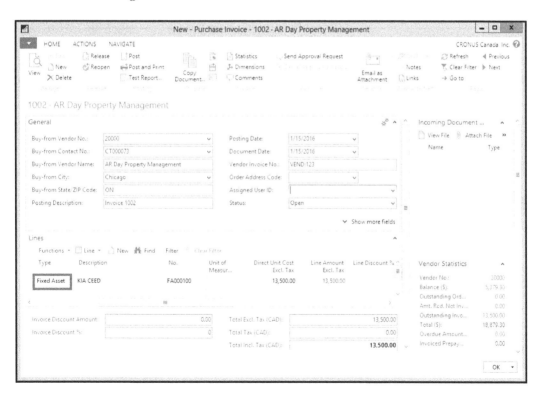

Revaluating fixed assets

In some cases, a fixed asset already exists and its acquisition cost has already been posted using a purchase invoice. Later on you need to increase the cost of the asset, because the company has invested additional costs into it, or for any other reason. To do so, you can use the **Fixed Assets G/L Journal** using the following steps:

You can use the journal even if no cost was posted earlier.

1. Navigate to `Fixed Assets/Fixed Assets G/L Journals`. Open the **DEFAULT** section by double-clicking on it.
2. Create a new line, similar to the one shown in the following screenshot. In this example, we are going to add `1000` to the cost of the asset. This includes taxes, which means that, once posted, only 800 will be added to the asset cost. Take a look at the following screenshot:

3. Post the journal lines, by selecting the **Post** option from the ribbon bar.
4. Go back to the **Fixed Asset Card** and note that the **Book Value** is now `14300`.

Calculating depreciation

Fixed assets reduce their value over time. We need to account for this fact by calculating and posting the fixed asset depreciation. Follow these steps to do so:

1. Run the **Calculate Depreciation** batch job by navigating to **Departments Financial** | **Management** | **Fixed Assets** | **Periodic Activities**.
2. Select the options shown in the following screenshot:

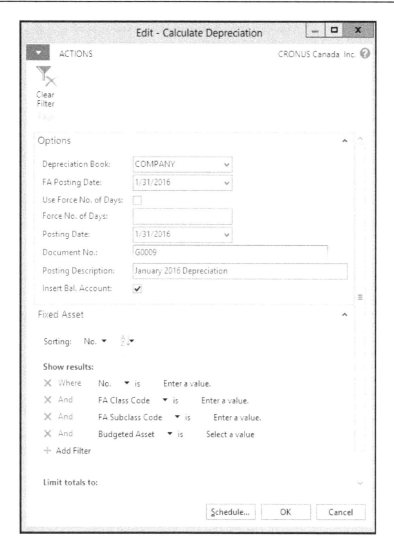

This job will calculate the depreciation for all the assets. In the example, we have filtered the job to only calculate the amounts for the **Fixed Asset No.:** FA000100. The system creates journal lines. You have to check and post them manually.

3. Navigate to **Fixed Assets** | **Fixed Assets G/L Journals**. Open the **DEFAULT** section by double-clicking on it. The program has created the following lines:

Batch Name:	DEFAULT								
Posting Date	Document Type	Document No.	Account Type	Account No.	Depreciation Book Code	FA Posting Type	Description	Amount	Bal. Account Type
1/31/2016		G0009	Fixed Asset	FA000100	COMPANY	Depreciation	January 2016 Depreciation	-129.00	G/L Account
1/31/2016		G0009	G/L Account	66300			January 2016 Depreciation	129.00	G/L Account

4. Post the lines.
5. Go back to the **Fixed Asset Card** and note that the **Book Value** is now `14173`.
6. Double-click on the **Book Value** to see the **FA Ledger Entries** for the asset.

For the asset we have created in this chapter, we selected the Straight-Line depreciation method. Dynamics NAV allows us to select one of the following depreciation methods:

Method	Definition
Straight-Line	The same amount is depreciated each year.
Declining-Balance 1	The largest portion of the cost is allocated to the early years of its useful lifetime. If you depreciate monthly, the same amount is depreciated for all the months in one year.
Declining-Balance 2	Similar to DB1, but if you depreciate monthly the depreciation amounts will decline for each period.
DB1/SL	DB1/SL stands for Declining-Balance 1 and Straight-Line. For each period, the greater of the two amounts is used to post the depreciation.
DB2/SL	It uses the same principle as DB1/SL, but the amounts are calculated according to the Declining-Balance 2 method.
User-defined	This allows you to define your own method.
Manual	You must enter the depreciation value manually.
Half-Year Convention	When Half-Year Convention is applied, a fixed asset will have six months' depreciation in the fiscal year. It can be used in conjunction with the Straight-Line, Declining-Balance 1, or DB1/SL methods.

Manually create depreciation lines

To manually create depreciation lines, access the journal and create one line similar to those the **Calculate Depreciation** batch job has created.

Dynamics NAV uses a standard year of 360 days and a standard month of 30 days for all calculations.

Selling or disposing of a fixed asset

Disposing of or selling a fixed asset is the last step in the typical life cycle of an asset. When you do so, you must post the disposal value together with any related gain or loss.

To sell the asset using a sales invoice, just create the invoice and select the **Fixed Asset** in one of the lines of the invoice, just like we did when purchasing the asset. Enter the selling price and post the invoice. The program will do the rest.

You can also post disposals using the **Fixed Assets G/L Journal**.

Canceling fixed asset entries

A batch job called **cancel FA entries** is used to cancel an incorrectly posted FA entry for one or more fixed assets. This task creates the new FA journal lines. When you post them, the system creates entries to nullify the incorrect ones, both on the general ledger and the FA ledger.

The depreciation for the asset FA00090 switchboard has already been calculated until December 2013. You have just realized that in October you had to add the cost to the asset. Therefore you need to cancel the depreciation until October, add the cost to the asset, and calculate the depreciation again. Let's see how you can cancel the depreciation entries:

1. Open the card of the asset FA00090 switchboard and click on the **Ledger Entries** option from the ribbon bar. The **FA Ledger Entries** page will open.
2. Select the entries you want to cancel. In the example, we are selecting the last three entries. That is the depreciation from October to December.
3. Click on the **Cancel Entries** option found on the ribbon bar. Click on **OK** on the emerging page.
4. Navigate to **Fixed Assets | Fixed Assets G/L Journals**. Open the **DEFAULT** section by double-clicking on it. The process has created journal lines that once posted will cancel the original depreciation entries.
5. Select all the journal lines and click on the **Insert FA Bal. Account** option. New lines will be inserted into the journal to balance the transaction.

6. Post the journal lines.
7. Go back to the **FA Ledger Entries** page and note that depreciation entries corresponding to October to December are not there anymore.

 Dynamics NAV does not delete any posted entry. The original depreciation entries have not been deleted, but unassigned. From the **Fixed Asset Card**, click on **Error Ledger Entries** on the **Navigate** tab of the ribbon bar, to see the original entries.

Inventory valuation

The valuation of your inventory must appear on your balance sheet accounts at the end of a fiscal year. The system can calculate the inventory valuation using different costing methods and can post it to the general ledger automatically, so that you do not have to worry about it. Due to performance issues, though, the inventory valuation is usually set up, so that posting to the general ledger is done manually.

Choosing a costing method

Dynamics NAV can calculate the valuation of your inventory according to five different costing methods: They are as follows:

- **First In First Out** (**FIFO**): It assumes that the first units to be received in your stock will also be the first ones that will leave it. The inventory valuation will be based on the cost of the last received units.
- **Last In First Out** (**LIFO**): It assumes that the last units to be received in your stock will be the first ones that will leave it. The inventory valuation will be based on the cost of the first received units.
- **Average**: The inventory valuation will be based on the average cost of all received units.
- **Specific**: This costing method can only be used when specific serial number tracking is done over the stock of the items. The inventory valuation will be based on the exact units that are in stock.
- **Standard**: This costing method does a FIFO calculation. The difference with FIFO is the way it takes incoming costs, which are based on an estimated cost that you set up on the item. This costing method is usually used for items that are manufactured.

The costing method is chosen at item level, so different items may use different costing methods.

 Study carefully which costing method you want to use. Once it is set and items have had any kind of movement, it cannot be changed.

Calculating item entry costs

Actually, you don't have to calculate anything. The system will do it for you. However, it is important to understand how costs are assigned to item entries.

The system assigns a cost to every single item entry. This is how different entry types get their cost:

Inbound entries

- **Purchases**: They first get an expected cost when the purchase receipt is posted. The expected cost is taken from the purchase order. When the invoice is posted, they get their real cost from the invoice.
- **Positive adjustments**: They have the cost that was specified on the item journal. By default, they get the actual average cost of the item, but can be changed by the user if needed.
- **Outputs of a manufacturing process**:
  - **Standard costing method**: They get the estimated cost defined on the item card
  - **Other costing methods**: Their cost is calculated as the sum of the costs of their components plus the cost of manufacturing the item

Outbound entries

The costing method used here determines how costs are assigned to outbound entries. They are always based on the costing of inbound entries for the same item, though.

This is not a complete list. There are other possibilities (such as an inbound entry as the result of a sales return) and different choices that can be made when manufacturing, for instance. We have just taken a look at the most common entries.

The costs in outbound entries are always based on the costs of inbound entries. What happens if the cost of the inbound entry changes after the cost has been assigned to the outbound entry? No problem, the cost in the outbound entry will be updated later on. This is actually done by a batch process called **Adjust Cost – Item Entries** that can be found by navigating to Financial Management/Inventory. You should run this process periodically to have your item costs up-to-date.

Posting an inventory valuation to the general ledger

Posting the inventory valuation to the general ledger will transfer the calculated item costs to the corresponding balance sheet account. To do so, we use the following steps:

1. Navigate to **Financial Management | Inventory** and select **Post Inventory Cost to G/L**.
2. Choose **Posting Method**, **Document No.**, and place a checkmark on **Post** as shown in the following screenshot:

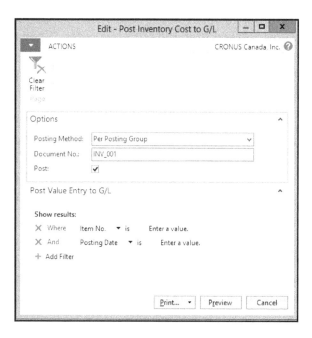

3. Click on **Preview**.
4. A report containing the posted costs will be shown.

Inventory valuation report

If you want to know your inventory valuation at a certain date, you have to run the **Inventory Valuation** report that can be found by navigating to `Financial Management/Inventory`. On this report, you can choose whether you want to include expected costs or not. Expected costs are those for item entries that have not yet been invoiced.

The printed report groups entries by inventory posting groups. The **Inventory Valuation** for January 2016 looks similar to the following screenshot:

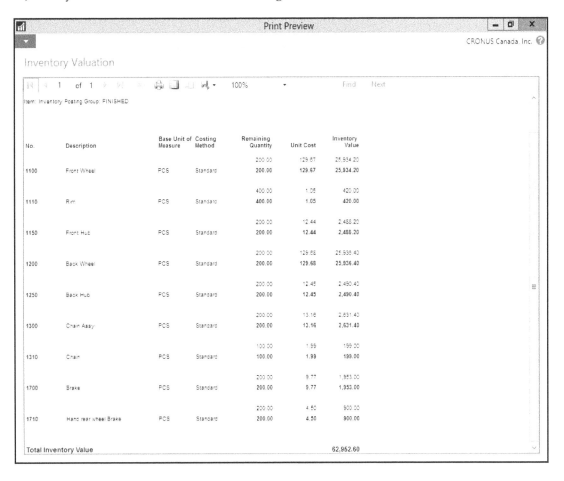

For each item, the report prints five groups of columns that shows the following information:

	Description
`As of`(beginning of the period)	This shows the quantity and value of the stock the day before the starting date is selected when running the period.
`Increases (LCY)`	This shows the quantity and value of the increases of stock for the given period. This includes purchases, positive adjustments, sale returns, manufactured items, and so on.
`Decreases (LCY)`	This shows the quantity and value of the decreases of stock for the given period. This includes sales, positive adjustments, purchase returns, consumed items, and so on.
`As of`(end of period)	This shows the quantity and value of the stock at the end of the period.
`Cost Posted to G/L`	This shows the cost that has already been posted to the general ledger.

Closing the accounting year

When a fiscal year reaches its end and accountants have finished posting all the needed transactions, it is time to perform the required tasks to close the year.

In Dynamics NAV, this can be accomplished in just a couple of steps: closing the accounting periods and running the **Close Income Statement** batch process. After that, it is advisable to restrict allowed posting dates to prevent users from posting any transaction in a closed year. If needed, though, further transactions can be posted.

Closing accounting periods

To close the accounting periods, we perform the following steps:

1. Navigate to **Financial Management** | **Periodic Activities** | **Fiscal Year** | **Accounting Periods**.
2. Run the **Close Year** process found on the ribbon.

3. You will be prompted to confirm that you want to close the fiscal year. You cannot choose which fiscal year to close. The system will close the first open fiscal year. Click on **Yes**. Refer to the following screenshot:

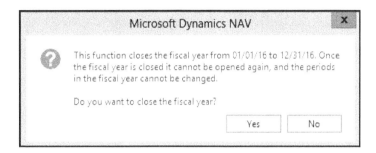

4. The fiscal year has been closed. Notice that all the accounting periods (which usually correspond to months) that have been closed now have a checkmark on the **Closed** and **Date Locked** fields.

Running the Close Income Statement batch process

At the end of each fiscal year, accounting rules specify that income account balances must be transferred to a balance sheet account. The **Close Income Statement** batch process is used to accomplish this task by calculating and creating the transaction that will transfer these balances. This process leaves the transaction on a general journal so that you can review and post it afterwards.

To run the **Close Income Statement** batch process, perform the following steps:

1. Navigate to `Financial Management/Periodic Activities/Fiscal Year` and click on **Close Income Statement**.
2. Choose which general journal and section you want to use (**Gen. Journal Template** and **Gen. Journal Batch** fields). This is where the transaction will be created.

3. Choose to which account the income account balances will be transferred. You do it by selecting an account on the **Retained Earnings Acc.** field as shown in the following screenshot:

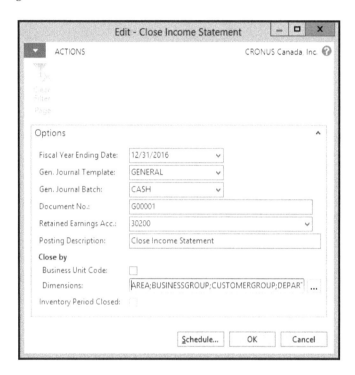

Even if not mandatory, if you use dimensions it is highly recommended you select them all when running the **Close Income Statement** batch process. If you choose not to do it, when running financial reports by dimensions, you will be carrying balances from one year to another because the closing transaction will not be posted using dimensions.

4. Click on **OK**.
5. Navigate to the journal you have chosen when running the process.
6. Notice that a special date is used in the **Close Income Statement**. It has the C letter in front of it and it is a closing date. It is a fictitious date between the last day of the old fiscal year and the first day of the new fiscal year. Using this kind of date, balances for the ordinary dates of the fiscal year are maintained. Take a look at the following screenshot:

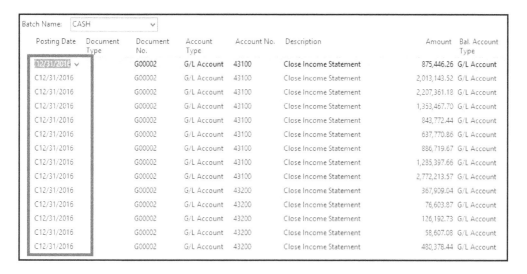

7. Post the journal.

Restricting allowed posting dates

It is highly recommended you restrict allowed posting dates after a period has been closed. That way, you prevent users from accidentally posting transactions to an incorrect date.

Posting dates can be restricted at the company level or at the user level.

 When both company and user restrictions exist, the ones that apply are the allowed posting dates defined at the user level.

To restrict allowed posting dates at the company level, navigate to **Financial Management | Administration** and click on **General Ledger Setup**. Use the **Allow Posting From** and **Allow Posting To** fields to specify the period in which it is allowed to post transactions as shown in the following screenshot:

To restrict allowed posting dates at the user level, navigate to **Administration** | **Application Setup** | **Users** and click on **User Setup**. Use the **Allow Posting From** and **Allow Posting To** fields to specify the period in which it is allowed to post transactions. Take a look at the following screenshot:

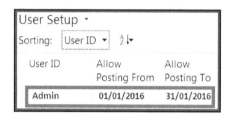

Posting transactions on a closed year

If the allowed posting dates allow you to, you can post transactions on a closed year. However, you will have to run the **Close Income Statement** batch process again. This process can be run as many times as needed.

Consolidating financial statements

When you have a group of companies, you may need to aggregate their financial statements into a single one to know how the holding company is doing as a group.

Such a task can be performed to consolidate different companies that are in the same database, companies in different databases (even in older Dynamics NAV versions), or using data coming from other business management programs.

Regarding data, consolidation can be performed when the different subsidiary companies or business units have different charts of accounts, fiscal years, or currencies.

Performing consolidation

Performing a consolidation is as easy as executing a batch process. There are different scenarios, though, depending on where the data is. The easiest scenario is when all the companies, including both the consolidated and the subsidiary companies, are on the same database. Another scenario includes Dynamics NAV companies on different databases. And a third scenario includes financial data from other applications. No matter which scenario you use, the consolidation process does the following actions:

- Transactions for each account in the subsidiary are totaled
- The net amounts are transferred to the corresponding accounts on the consolidated company
- Residual amounts are posted in the consolidated company due to rounding differences that may occur when a subsidiary is partially consolidated (only the percentage in which the holding company participates on the subsidiary company is consolidated)

The consolidation can be performed as many times as needed. If a transaction for the same subsidiary and period already exists in the consolidated database, the existing transaction is voided (its amount is set to zero). This way, the consolidated company will only take into account the information from the last executed consolidation.

Consolidating on a single database

To consolidate multiple subsidiaries that are on the same database, we perform the following steps:

1. Open the consolidated company.
2. Navigate to **Financial Management** | **PeriodicActivities** | **Consolidation** | **Business Units**.
3. On the **ACTIONS** tab, click on **Import Database....**

4. Specify the consolidation period and a document number for the consolidated transactions as shown in the following screenshot:

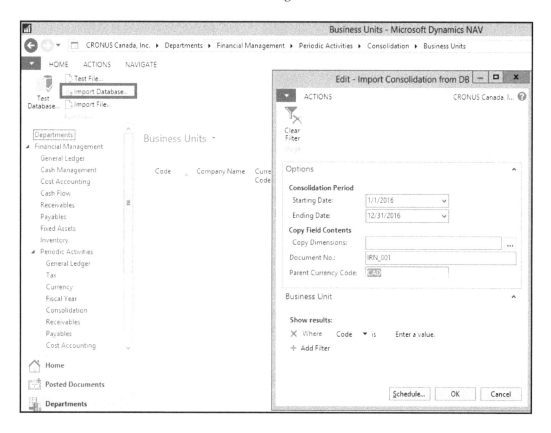

5. Click on **OK**.

Consolidating with different databases

When you consolidate subsidiary companies that are on different databases, you have to first export the financial data of each subsidiary and then import it into the consolidated company.

To export the financial data from each subsidiary, perform the following actions on every single subsidiary company:

1. Open the subsidiary company.
2. Navigate to **Financial Management** | **Periodic Activities** | **Consolidation** and click on **Export Consolidation**.
3. Select the **Consolidation Period** and the file format. The file format depends on the version of Dynamics NAV that the consolidated company uses. Take a look at the following screenshot:

4. Click on **OK.**
5. Save the file. You will need this file later on.

To import the data into the consolidated company, perform the following actions for each file exported previously:

1. Open the consolidated company.
2. Navigate to **Financial Management** | **Periodic Activities** | **Consolidation** | **Business Units**.
3. On the **ACTIONS** tab, click on **Import Database**.
4. Specify the file format you have used when exporting data from a subsidiary and the document number for the consolidated transactions.
5. Click on **OK**.
6. Select the file you have exported previously.

Consolidating with other applications

To consolidate subsidiaries that use other business management applications, you need to first export data from the business management application and then import it in the consolidated company in Dynamics NAV, just as when consolidating subsidiaries that are in different databases.

The other applications should be able to export data in the same format as Dynamics NAV, which can be either a `.txt` or an `.xml` file.

Reporting over a consolidated company

Any of the existing financial reports can be used to report over a consolidated company. Additionally, though, there is a **Consolidated Trial Balance** that shows the individual amounts of each subsidiary company and the total, taking them all into account.

This report can be executed from any business unit card.

Setting it up

Setting everything up is the tough part of consolidation. But this is something that has to be done just once, so it's worth the effort.

Financial consolidation is usually done into a company created and configured for this single purpose. This company will not hold normal business transactions.

To set up financial consolidation, you need to perform the following tasks:

1. Create a new empty company. It will be the consolidated company.
2. Create the chart of accounts on that company. The consolidated chart of accounts can be different from the one used in subsidiary companies. Subsidiary companies can each have their own different chart of accounts.
3. On the consolidated company, specify the business units (subsidiary companies) that we will be consolidating.
4. On each subsidiary company, define the translation between its chart of accounts and the consolidated chart of accounts.

Dimensions can be used when consolidating. We haven't yet explained what dimensions are, so we will skip this part for now.

Defining business units

Business units are the subsidiary companies that will be used in a consolidated company. They can be found by navigating to **Financial Management** | **Periodic Activities** | **Consolidation** | **Business Units**. The following screenshot shows a **Business Unit Card** page:

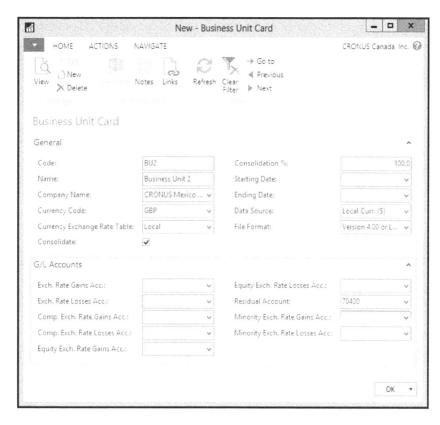

When defining a business unit, you need to specify a **Code** and a **Name** as well:

- **Company Name**: This is to specify where the business unit is created, in Dynamics NAV or in other business management applications.
- **Currency Code**: This is used to specify if the subsidiary company uses a different currency than the consolidated company. Also which exchange rate to use (the one defined on the subsidiary or the one defined on the consolidated company).
- **Consolidation %**: This number represents the participation that the holding or group has over the subsidiary company. When the **Consolidation %** is 50, for instance, only half of the balance of that subsidiary will be consolidated.

- **G/L Accounts**: This is where transactions will be posted on the consolidated company because of currency differences or residual amounts that may occur because of the percentage used on the consolidation.

Translating a chart of accounts

On each subsidiary, we need to specify the translation between the chart of accounts of that company and the chart of accounts defined on the consolidated company. The translation is done on each G/L account card, on the **Consolidation** FastTab. You can define different destiny accounts for debit and credit balances.

Take a look at the following screenshot:

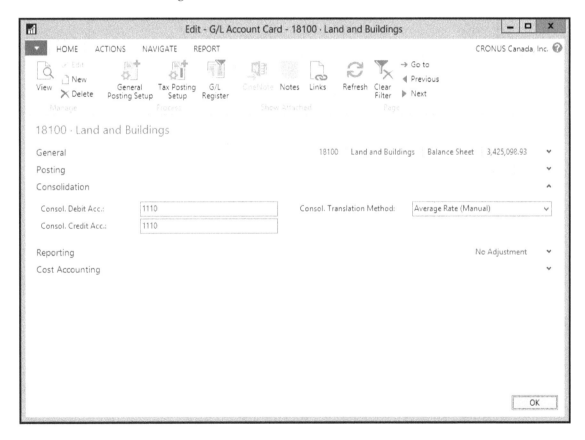

Deferrals

Deferrals are used to record revenues and expenses in periods other than the period where we have posted the transactions.

Setups that you are required to perform are as follows:

- The main account setup for **Deferral Account** (Balance sheet) where deferred revenues are posted, when you post a sales invoice for services delivered over a span of multiple accounting periods. Refer to the following screenshot:

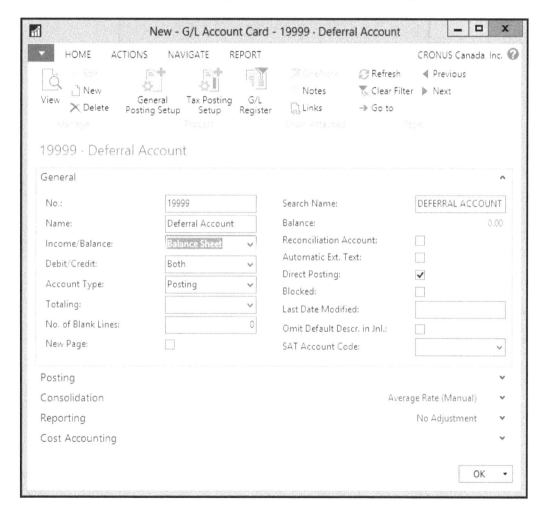

- The deferral template setup is where you can define **Deferral Account**, **No. of Periods**, **Calc.Meth...**, **Start Date**, and so on as shown in the following screenshot:

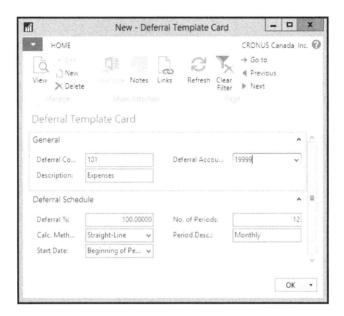

- Assign the deferral template to **Resource**, as follows:

- Record the sales invoice and view the deferral transactions as follows:

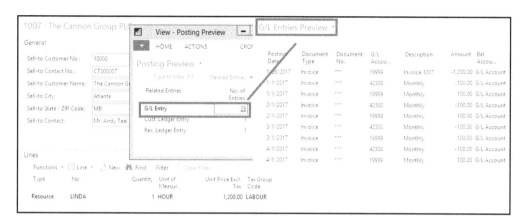

Summary

In this chapter, we learned how to post any accountancy transaction using journals. We explored how VAT entries are created when taxes are involved and how we can use them to report taxes to the authorities. We saw how to create a fixed asset and post its acquisition cost, revaluate it, calculate its depreciation, sell it, or cancel wrong entries.

In the annual accounting close section, we have learned the steps we need to perform in order to close the fiscal year, and in the inventory valuation section we came across different costing methods and how to reflect item costs into the general ledger. Finally, we have seen how to perform the consolidation of different subsidiary companies.

In the next chapter, we will take a look at the reporting tools available in Dynamics NAV. This way we will be able to analyze all the data collected in the system.

4
Reporting and Business Intelligence

So far we have seen the data entry and data process side of Dynamics NAV in the previous chapters. Once data is introduced into the system, you should be able to analyze it.

Are our departments generating value for the company? Which items or services are the most profitable? What area is experiencing a bigger sales growth? Analysis and reporting can help you to answer these questions.

In this chapter, we will see the tools available to analyze Dynamics NAV data, both inside and outside the application. This chapter covers the following topics:

- Dimensions
- Filters, charts, and statistics
- Reports
- Account schedules
- Analysis views
- Business Intelligence with Excel and PowerPivot

Understanding dimensions

The term dimension is used to describe how analysis occurs. A two-dimensional analysis, for example, would be sales per area. In a more complex scenario, we could also analyze sales per sales campaign, per customer group, and per area.

In order to be able to analyze those dimensions you have to make sure that each and every single entry contains the information needed. In Dynamics NAV, a dimension can be seen as information linked to an entry, such as a tag or a characteristic. The purpose of dimensions is to group entries with similar characteristics so that you can report on the data in a way that is meaningful to the company.

You can define your own dimensions according to how you need to analyze your data. Each dimension can have unlimited dimension values that are subunits of the dimension. For example, a dimension called `Department` can have subunits called `Sales`, `Administration`, and so on. These departments are dimension values.

In Dynamics NAV, you can create unlimited dimensions. However, there are some restrictions on how to access their information. We can group dimensions in three categories, according to their access level (how easy is to access them):

- **Global dimensions**: It is very easy to access and filter on them. We can use up to two global dimensions.
- **Shortcut dimensions**: You need to open a separate page to access them. On some occasions, they are shown on the page's journal and document pages to make it easier to introduce them. We can use up to eight shortcut dimensions. Two of them correspond to global dimensions.
- **The rest of the dimensions**: You always need to open a separate page to introduce or see them.

Defining default dimensions on master data

Imagine you want to analyze your sales according to the size of your customers. You create a dimension called **CUSTOMERGROUP** and you define different dimension values such as **LARGE**, **MEDIUM**, and **SMALL**.

One customer might only be a part of one of those groups, so you inform him/her as a default dimension for the customer. You can do this using the following steps:

1. Navigate to **Departments** | **Sales & Marketing** | **Sales** | **Customers**.
2. Select the `01905902, London Candoxy Storage Campus` customer, and click on the Dimensions/Dimensions-single icon on the ribbon bar. The **Default Dimensions** page opens.

3. Create a new line for the **CUSTOMERGROUP** dimension, as shown in the following screenshot:

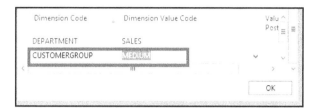

Now, every time you post a new invoice for the customer or use the customer in documents or journals, the default dimensions defined will be used.

 Default dimensions can be defined in all master data such as customers, vendors, G/L accounts, items, resources, fixed assets, and so on.

Using dimensions on documents and journals

On some occasions, the default dimensions are not enough and you need to inform about dimensions on single documents or on single journal lines. Let's see it with an example:

1. Create a new sales invoice for customer `01905902, London Candoxy Storage Campus`.
2. Click on the Dimensions icon found on the ribbon bar. The **Dimension Set Entries** page opens.
3. The default dimensions defined for the customer and the salesperson have already been transferred to the document. Create a new line for the **SALESCAMPAIGN** dimension, as shown in the following screenshot:

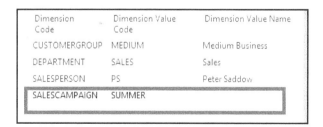

Once you post the invoice, all the resulting entries will have all four dimensions associated to it.

> In the example, we have added a new dimension, but you can also delete one of the default dimensions transferred or change its value for this single invoice.

In the example, we have set dimension values for the entire document, but it is also possible to set dimension values at the document-line level.

Using filters and flowfilters

A good and powerful way to view and analyze data is to use filters and flowfilters inside the application. Both of them are used to narrow down the information seen on screen or the information a report produces. Filters can be applied on all pages and on most of the reports. In this section, we will see how to apply filters and flowfilters on pages. In the *Using reports* section, we will see how to apply them on reports.

Applying filters on pages

The filtering pane can be found on the upper part of the page, as shown in the following screenshot:

There is a quick filter section in the upper-right corner where filters can be applied over any of the fields that are shown on-screen. Filters can also be applied over two or more fields at a time, or over fields that are not shown on-screen. To do so, the **Advanced Filter** section should be shown by clicking on the down arrow found at the right of the **Quick Filter** section. A **Show results:** subsection should be shown on-screen, similar to the following screenshot:

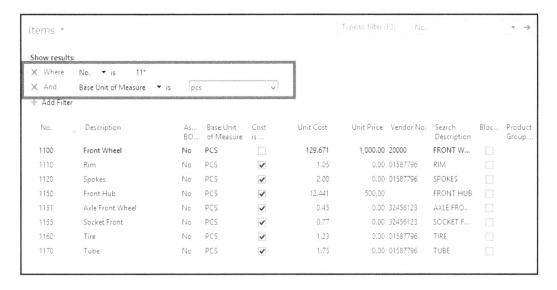

In the **Advanced Filter** section, you can select any field to filter, and you can also add new filters.

Imagine that on the item list we want to see all items that have a unit cost **>=100** and whose vendor number is vendor **20000** or vendor **30000**. We can see only those items by applying filters over the **Unit Cost** and the **Vendor No.** fields, as shown in the following screenshot:

There are multiple filtering expressions that can be used, including operators (>, <, and =), statements (| and &), or intervals, compound expressions, and so on.

 For a complete list of available filtering expressions, refer to the online documentation found at `https://msdn.microsoft.com/en-us/library/hh879066(v=nav.90).aspx`.

Applying flowfilters on pages

Flowfilters are a special type of filter that isn't used to narrow down results but to narrow down calculations. Some of the information you see in the application is actually a calculation based on other information. For instance, the balance for customers and vendors is actually a calculation based on their ledger entries. So are inventories on items or the balance on general ledger accounts.

Let's see how to apply a flowfilter on the chart of accounts and the result it produces. We will perform the following steps:

1. Open the chart of accounts by navigating to **Department** | **Financial Management** | **General Ledger** | **Chart of Accounts**.
2. On this page, the **Net Change** and **Balance** fields show the sum of general ledger entry amounts for the different accounts.
3. Click on **Chart of Accounts** and select **Limit totals to:**.
4. Add a filter for **Date Filter** and set it as `01/01/16..12/31/16`.
5. The **Net Change** field will be updated. When no flowfilter was applied, both **Net Change** and **Balance** were showing the same amounts. Refer to the following screenshot:

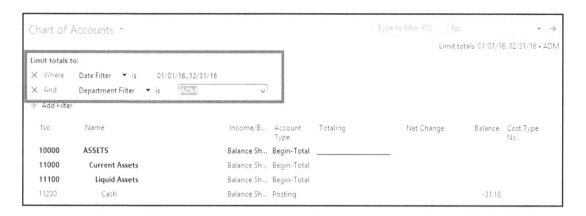

Not all flowfilters apply to all flowfields. In the example, we have seen that, after applying a date flowfilter, the **Net Change** field gets updated and shows only the sum of G/L entry amounts of the specified period, while the **Balance** field has remained the same. This is because of the definition of the fields. The definition of the **Net Change** field states that the calculation for this field will take into account a date filter, while the **Balance** field does not.

Creating views

We have seen how to apply filters and flowfilters on pages. But if we leave the page and open it again later on, the filter is gone. We have to apply the same filter or flowfilter over and over again if we want to see the same results. Wouldn't it be great if we could save the filters so that we could apply them as many times as we wish without having to select again the fields we want to filter and writing the filter expression? That is possible by saving views.

To save a view, perform the following steps:

1. Follow the steps mentioned in the previous section to apply filters on the item list page.
2. Click on **Items** and select **Save View As...**.

3. Specify a **Name** for the view and select the **Activity Group** in which you want to save your view, as shown in the following screenshot:

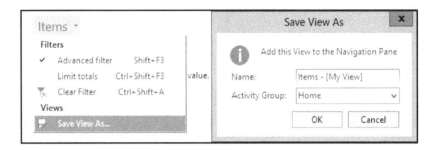

Every time you want to see your saved view, follow the given steps:

1. Click on **Home** (or on the **Activity Group** in which you have saved your view).
2. Click on your saved view.

Using reports

Dynamics NAV has a bunch of reports that can be used out-of-the-box. Some other reports may have been added by a partner and can also be used.

Most reports can be found under the Reports and Analysis category on all functional areas. They can also be found in many application pages, where only the reports that are valid for the data shown on the page will be found.

When running a report, the request page for the report will usually be shown. On the request page, you can usually specify different options. You can apply filters to narrow down the information that will be shown or processed and you can choose whether to preview the report or print it to different devices or applications (use a printer or print to PDF, Excel, or Word).

In the following screenshot, you can see the request page for the **Customer Top 10 List** report:

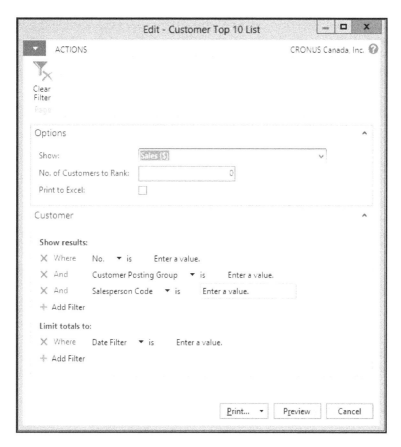

Not all the reports have an options section and not all reports allow filters to be applied. Whenever these happen, the corresponding sections will not be shown.

Displaying charts

Graphical information is always useful when analyzing data. Dynamics NAV offers various ways of viewing data in a graphical way.

The show as chart option

Whenever the information shown on the screen can be viewed as a chart, on the **Home** tab of the ribbon you will see a section called **View** where users can switch the view of the information from list to chart and vice versa as shown in the following screenshot:

When you switch to chart view, you can select which fields you want to use as a measure and which ones you want to use as dimensions.

Adding charts to the Role Center page

Dynamics NAV has a set of predefined charts that can be added to the **Role Center** page. To add a chart to the home page, perform the following steps:

1. Click on **Home**.
2. Click on the Application icon ![icon], click on **Customize**, and then click on **Customize This Page**.
3. Select **Chart Part** from the **Available parts** column and click on the **Add** button.
4. A **Blank Chart** will appear in the **Role Center layout** column.
5. Select **Blank Chart** and click on the **Customize Part** button.
6. Select one of the available charts.
7. Click on **OK** to close the **Customize the Role Center** window

Back on the **Role Center** page, you will see the chosen chart displayed.

If the predefined generic charts are not enough for you, you can define your own generic charts and make them available to all users. To do so, navigate to **Department** | **Administration** | **Application Setup** | **RoleTailored Client** | **Generic Charts** and create your chart by specifying the information it should display.

Using account schedules

The account schedule functionality is part of the *Analysis & Reporting* section of the **Financial Management** area. It is meant to create customized financial reports based on general ledger information, budget information, or on the analysis views information. Account schedules can group data from various accounts and perform calculations that are not possible directly on the chart of accounts.

When defining account schedules, the information that will be displayed on both rows and columns can be defined.

Just to see how it works, we will create a simple account schedule that will compare budgeted amounts versus real amounts. To do so, we perform the following steps:

1. Navigate to **Departments** | **Financial Management** | **Reports and Analysis and choose Account Schedules**.
2. Click on **New** to create a new account schedule. For the new account schedule, select **EXAMPLE** as the **Name**, **Comparing budget versus reality** as the **Description**, and **ACT/BUD** as the **Default Column Layout**.
3. Click on **Account Schedule**.
4. Define the account schedule as shown in the following screenshot:

5. The rows in the screenshot mean the following:
    - The first row gets the net amount of account 69950, a totaling account that summarizes all operating expenses.
    - On the second row, a formula sums the results of rows 3 and 4.
    - The third row gets the net amount of other expenses from the posting accounts 64300 and 67500. As this row is only used for calculation purposes and to show on the report, the **Show** field has been set to Yes.

- The fourth row gets the net amount of other expenses from the totaling accounts. The totaling accounts used are 67000 and 67600. The **Show** field has been set to Yes.

The account schedule is fully defined now. The account schedule defines the rows that will be shown on the report. Columns are defined in the **Column Layout** page. In the example, we have used an existing column layout called **ACT/BUD**. Let's see what the following column layout will show:

1. On the **Account Schedule** page where we were defining our account schedule, click on the **Actions** tab and then click on **Edit Colum Layout Setup**.
2. Select **ACT/BUD** for the **Name** field. The **ACT/BUD** column layout definition will be shown. Refer to the following screenshot:

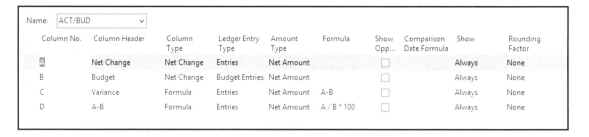

Name:	ACT/BUD								
Column No.	Column Header	Column Type	Ledger Entry Type	Amount Type	Formula	Show Opp...	Comparison Date Formula	Show	Rounding Factor
A	Net Change	Net Change	Entries	Net Amount		☐		Always	None
B	Budget	Net Change	Budget Entries	Net Amount		☐		Always	None
C	Variance	Formula	Entries	Net Amount	A-B	☐		Always	None
D	A-B	Formula	Entries	Net Amount	A / B * 100	☐		Always	None

3. The column layout defines that the report will have four columns called **Net Change**, **Budget**, **Variance**, and **A-B**:
    - The **Net Change** column will show the net amount for G/L entries
    - The **Budget** column will show the net amount for budget entries
    - The **Variance** column will show the difference between the first and the second column
    - The **A-B** column calculates the percentage that the first column represents versus the second column

Now that we have defined both the account schedule and the column layout, it is time to see the results of our account schedule.

1. Navigate to **Departments** | **Financial Management** | **Reports and Analysis and choose Account Schedules**. Select the one we have just created.
2. Click on **Overview**. The report will be shown on screen, similar to the following screenshot:

 The results can be seen in different time periods and filters can be applied over the calculation to get more accurate results. The results can be exported to Excel and can also be printed.

Analysis views

Analysis views are used to analyze information about dimensions from General Ledger entries, budgets, and cash flow forecast entries. As we have seen, not all dimensions are easily accessed. Analysis views are meant to access all the dimensions in the same easy way, in groups of a maximum of four dimensions at the same time. The four dimension groups may seem a limitation but aren't, since we can create as many analysis views as needed, combining all the dimensions we want.

Creating an analysis view

Follow the given steps to create an analysis view:

1. Navigate to **Departments** | **Administration** | **Application Setup** | **Financial Management** | **Dimensions** | **Analysis Views**. The **Analysis Views** page will open showing the existing analysis views.

2. Click on an existing analysis view. View the analysis view card with the data shown in the following screenshot:

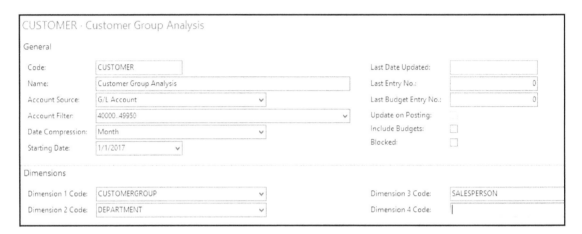

3. Click on the **Update** option found on the ribbon bar to create analysis views entries based on the criteria that you set up on the card.

The system will create one summarized analysis view entry for each G/L account, period, and dimension combination.

In the example, we will get one entry for each G/L account from **Account Filter 40000..49950**, for each month and also for each combination of dimension values of the **CUSTOMERGROUP**, **DEPARTMENT**, and **SALESPERSON** dimensions.

4. Navigate to **Departments** ⏐ **Financial Management** ⏐ **General Ledger** ⏐ **History** ⏐ **Analysis View Entries** to see the entries created by the system.

An analysis view is a fixed photo of the posted G/L entries grouped with specific criteria. Therefore, if you change any of the fields of the card (that is, the criteria are changed), the system will prompt you to delete the analysis entries and update them again.

You will also have to use the Update action to include new general ledger entries posted after you last updated the analysis view. However, you can also let the system update them automatically when new G/L entries are posted, by checking the **Update on Posting:** field found on the analysis view card.

It is not recommended to use the **Update on Posting:** option because it penalizes performance when posting.

Using analysis views

Analysis views can be used in the analysis by dimensions functionality or as a source of account schedules. In this section, we are going to follow an example of each.

Analysis by dimensions

The analysis by dimensions functionality is used to display and analyze the amount derived from the existing analysis views. To set an example, perform the following steps:

1. Navigate to **Departments** ⏐ **Financial Management** ⏐ **General Ledger** ⏐ **Analysis & Reporting** ⏐ **Analysis by Dimensions**.
2. Locate the CUST.REVEN analysis view that we have created earlier in this chapter. Then click on **Edit Analysis View** from the ribbon bar.
3. A new page opens. Type LARGE in the **CUSTOMERGROUP Filter** field.

4. Click on the Show Matrix icon found on the ribbon bar. The **Analysis by Dimensions Matrix** page now shows the amounts posted on the general ledger under the **LARGE** value of the **CUSTOMERGROUP** dimension. Refer to the following screenshot:

Analysis by Dimensions Matrix ▾				
Code	Name	Total Amount	01/01/17	02/01/17
42000	**Sales of Resources**			
42100	Sales, Resources - Dom.			
42200	Sales, Resources - EU			
42300	Sales, Resources - Export	-45,508.00	-45,508.00	
42400	Job Sales Adjmt., Resources			
42500	**Total Sales of Resources**	**-45,508.00**	**-45,508.00**	
43000	**Sales of Raw Materials**			
43100	Sales, Raw Materials - Dom.	-303.00	-303.00	
43200	Sales, Raw Materials - EU	-28,050.54	-28,050.54	
43300	Sales, Raw Materials - Export	-837.00	-837.00	
43400	Job Sales Adjmt., Raw Mat.			
43500	**Total Sales of Raw Materials**	**-29,190.54**	**-29,190.54**	

5. Close the current page and go back to the **Analysis by Dimensions** page.
6. Select different values for the following fields, and click on **Show Matrix** to see the results. The main fields you can change to analyze data are **Show as Lines**, **Show as Columns**, **Dimension Filters**, **Show**, **Show Amount Field**, **View by**, and **View as**.

Analysis views as a source of account schedules

If analysis views are selected as source for account schedules, the amounts in the account schedules are calculated based on analysis view entries. Since analysis view entries are based on the general ledger entries, the result should be the same.

The difference is that, when analyzing account schedules, you can only filter the amounts based on global dimensions. But if you use analysis views as the source, then you can filter on any of the four dimensions selected on the analysis view card. These dimensions can be global dimensions, shortcut dimensions, or any other dimensions. To use analysis views as the source for account schedules, perform the following steps:

1. Navigate to **Departments** | **Financial Management** | **General Ledger** | **Analysis & Reporting** | **Account Schedules**.

2. Locate the **REVENUE** account schedule. Notice that an analysis view is selected in the **Analysis View Name** field. This is what makes it possible to use the analysis view as the source for the account schedule. Refer to the following screenshot:

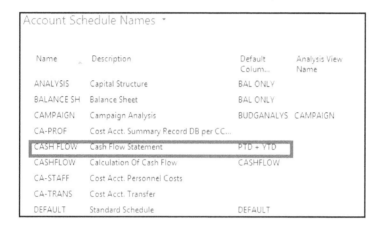

3. Click on the **Overview** option found on the ribbon bar. The **Acc. Schedule Overview** page opens. Notice that you can now filter on any of the three dimensions that were set up on the analysis view. Select different values on those fields to see the results as shown in the following screenshot:

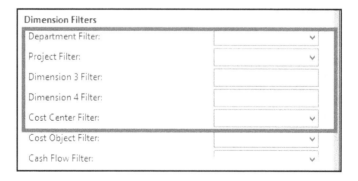

Business Intelligence with Excel and PowerPivot

With Dynamics NAV, we can easily create our own report in Microsoft Excel using **Business Intelligence** (**BI**) tools. Let's create a report to analyze the total sales and profits, grouped per customer or per item:

1. Open Excel. On the **PowerPivot** tab, click on the **PowerPivot Window** option.
2. A new page opens. Navigate to **From database** | **SQL database**. Type the server and database name of your Dynamics NAV. Click on **Next**.
3. Choose the **Select in the table and views list to choose data to import option**.
4. From the table and views list, select the following tables:

Table Name	Comments
CRONUS International Ltd_$Value Entry	Click on **Preview & Filters**. Filter the **Item Ledg. Entry Type** field to only show lines with the value 1.
CRONUS International Ltd_$Item	
CRONUS International Ltd_$Customer	

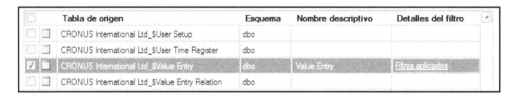

5. Click on **Finish**. Then click on **Close**. Close the **PowerPivot Window** to go back to the Excel sheet.
6. Now that we have selected the data source, let's create a Pivot table. To do so, click on the **Pivot table** option of Excel. Select **New Sheet** and click on **OK**.

7. On the PowerPivot fields list, select the fields as shown in the following screenshot. If the message **A relation may be needed** appears, click on **Create**. The power pivot table will show the sales grouped by customer and item, as shown in the following screenshot:

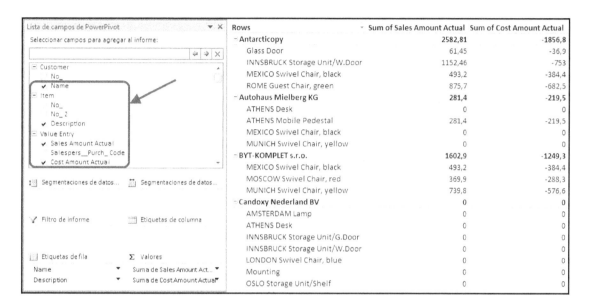

Rows	Sum of Sales Amount Actual	Sum of Cost Amount Actual
− Antarcticopy	2582,81	-1856,8
Glass Door	61,45	-36,9
INNSBRUCK Storage Unit/W.Door	1152,46	-753
MEXICO Swivel Chair, black	493,2	-384,4
ROME Guest Chair, green	875,7	-682,5
− Autohaus Mielberg KG	281,4	-219,5
ATHENS Desk	0	0
ATHENS Mobile Pedestal	281,4	-219,5
MEXICO Swivel Chair, black	0	0
MUNICH Swivel Chair, yellow	0	0
− BYT-KOMPLET s.r.o.	1602,9	-1249,3
MEXICO Swivel Chair, black	493,2	-384,4
MOSCOW Swivel Chair, red	369,9	-288,3
MUNICH Swivel Chair, yellow	739,8	-576,6
− Candoxy Nederland BV	0	0
AMSTERDAM Lamp	0	0
ATHENS Desk	0	0
INNSBRUCK Storage Unit/G.Door	0	0
INNSBRUCK Storage Unit/W.Door	0	0
LONDON Swivel Chair, blue	0	0
Mounting	0	0
OSLO Storage Unit/Shelf	0	0

Now, we can use the pivot table options and add more fields on rows, filters, segmentation, and so on.

Once we have created our Excel pivot table, we can save it, and open it again later. We will only have to refresh the PowerPivot source to get the latest data; we will not have to create the report all over again.

> Using PowerPivot, the source of data is always Dynamics NAV. Data does not get copied from the database to Excel, so no duplication exists.

Summary

In this chapter, we have learned what dimensions are and we have seen that they are a tool for tagging all our ledger entries. They allow you to analyze the data saved in the system in a manner that is useful to your company. We have learned to analyze data on screen, using filters, flowfilters, and charts. We have also learned about reports, an out of the box way of analyzing data. Account schedules are a tool that helps us analyze data from ledger entries, and so are analysis views. Analysis views are also useful to analyze financial groups by dimensions. Finally, we saw how to link Excel with our Dynamics NAV database to be able to use the Business Intelligence tools included in Excel.

In the next chapter, we are going to take a look at different predictive tools included in Dynamics NAV, such as budgets or cash flow foretelling.

5
Foretelling - Budgeting and Cash Flow Management

Accounting rules are based on *faits accomplis* but companies need to anticipate/predict events. Dynamics NAV offers some tools that can help to accomplish this, which we will cover in this chapter:

- Budgets
- Cash flow management

Budgets

Budgets are an overview of planned costs, revenues, and resources over a specified period of time. Dynamics NAV allows you to create budgets for fixed assets, items, sales and purchases, and projects. But we will focus on general ledger budgets in this section.

With the general ledger budget feature, you can create multiple budgets for the same time periods, simple or complex budgets by selecting combinations of G/L accounts, periods, and dimensions. You can also copy budgets from previous periods or create your budgets outside the application, with Excel, and then import it into Dynamics NAV.

Creating budgets

Let's create a new budget for the first quarter of 2017. Perform the following steps:

1. In the **Search** box, type `G/L Budgets` and select the related link.
2. Once on the **G/L Budgets** page, click on **New** on the ribbon bar. Create a new budget with the values shown in the following screenshot:

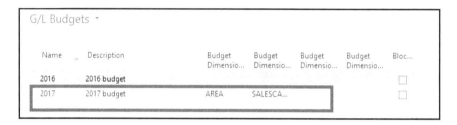

3. Click on the **Edit Budget** option found on the ribbon bar.
4. In the **View by** field, select **Month**.
5. In the **Data Filter:** field, write `01/01/17.12/31/17`.
6. We will enter the sales budget for the **SALES** department for the **MERCEDES** project, so add these dimensions as filters:

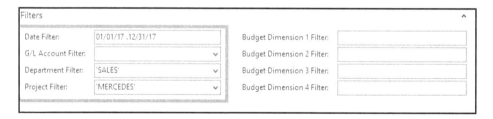

7. In the **Budget Matrix** tab, type in the budget amounts for each period, as shown in the following screenshot:

Budget Matrix

— Balance ▾   🔍 Find   Filter   ⌦ Clear Filter

Code	Name	Budgeted Amount	Jan 2017	Feb 2017	Mar 2017	Apr 2017
44000	**Sales of Retail**					
44100	Sales, Retail - Dom.	16,500.00	5,000.00	5,500.00	6,000.00	...
44200	Sales, Retail - EU					
44300	Sales, Retail - Export					
44399	Job Sales Applied, Retail					
44400	Job Sales Adjmt., Retail					
44500	**Total Sales of Retail**	16,500.00	5,000.00	5,500.00	6,000.00	
45000	Consulting Fees - Dom.					

 When you type in the amounts in the **Budget Matrix** tab, the system creates **G/L Budget Entries** with the given information. You can view them by double-clicking on the **Budgeted Amount** field for account number **44110**.

8. Leave the **Filter** field empty. Then double-click on the **Budgeted Amount** field for the account **44110**.

9. On the **G/L Budget Entries** page, create the following lines:

10. Back to the budget page, you will see that the created lines are summarized in the corresponding periods. You can refer to the **Budget Matrix** page.

11. Remove the filter from the **Department Filter** field.

12. Click on the **Copy Budget** option from the ribbon bar. To run the **Copy G/L Budget** job, select the following options, as shown in the following screenshot:

13. We have filtered the **G/L Account No.** field to only include the two accounts we were working on. In the **Date** field, we have selected the same period from the previous year. Therefore, in the **Date Change Formula:** input box, type 1Y in order to add one year to the dates. We are creating budgets for the **CUSTOMERGROUP** and **AREA** dimensions, so we have checked them on the **Dimensions** field.

14. Finally, we want to apply a 10% of sales increment, so we choose 1.1 as the adjustment factor. We choose to compress movements on a monthly basis and to round amounts to hundreds.

14. Click on **OK**. The system will create new budget entries based on real general ledger entries from previous periods. We have already created the budget for two different areas. For the rest of the areas, we will create an Excel template and ask the area director to fill in the budget for us. Then, we will import the Excel sheets to complete our budget.

16. Click on the **Export to Excel** option from the ribbon bar. Run the report with the following options:

Field	Value
Start Date	01/01/2017
No. of Periods	3
Period Length	1M
Column Dimensions	CUSTOMERGROUP; DEPARTMENT
G/L Account No.	41100

17. The director of the America area has filled in the following Excel sheet:

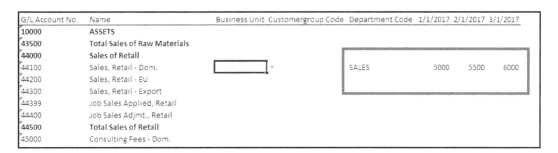

18. On the budget page, select the **Import from Excel** option from the ribbon bar and select the Excel file.
19. Select **Add entries** in the **Option** field and click on **OK**.
20. The system will create new budget entries based on the amounts introduced in the Excel template.

Using budgets

You have already seen three methods to create budgets. Now, we will see when budgets can be used. Budgets are mainly to compare reality versus budgeted amounts to measure performance. Budget entries can be also used as a source for the cash flow management. We will cover those in the next section.

The **Trial Balance/Budget** report, found under **Departments** | **Financial Management** | **General Ledger** | **Reports** | **Financial Statement**, compares the balance of each account in the charts of accounts with its budgeted amount for a given period.

You can also use budgets on **Account Schedules** to measure performance in an aggregate way. In the **Column Layout** definition, in the **Ledger Entry type** field, you can select the **Budget Entries** value to base the calculation on budget entries. To see an example, navigate to **Departments** | **Financial Management** | **Setup** | **General** | **Column Layouts** and analyze the definition of the **ACT/BUD** column layout.

Cash flow management

Understanding the flow of incoming and outstanding cash is vital for any company. We need to know if we will have enough money to pay creditors and expenses when they are due. This is actually what the cash flow management functionality will tell us. We will see how to do this in this section.

The cash flow management functionalities analyze several sources of information to be able to predict cash needs. The sources that this functionality uses are as follows:

- **General ledger**: This uses information about the liquid funds and also about the budgets we have seen in the previous section
- **Purchases**: This uses information about the current payables and also forecasted information taken from open purchase orders
- **Sales**: This uses information about the current receivables and also forecasted information taken from open sales orders
- **Service**: This uses information about open service orders
- **Fixed assets**: This uses information about planned disposal and budgeted purchases of fixed assets
- **Manual revenues and expenses**: This can also use information that we can set up manually, such as salaries, interest on credits, private consumptions, and so on

Let's see how it works by creating a cash flow forecast:

1. Navigate to **Departments** | **Financial Management** | **Cash Flow** | **Cash Flow Forecasts**.
2. Click on **New** to create a new cash flow forecast.
3. Press the *Enter* key. The system will give a number to the new forecast.

4. Enter the information shown in the following screenshot:

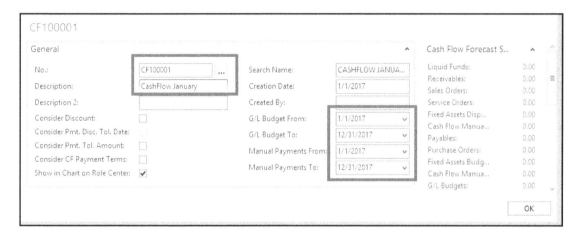

5. Close the cash flow forecast card.

We have created a forecast and we have set up the basic information about it. The next step is to obtain cash information from the system and bring it to our forecast. To do so, perform the following steps:

1. Navigate to **Departments** | **Financial Management** | **Cash Flow** | **Cash Flow Worksheet**.
2. Click on **Suggest Worksheet Lines**.
3. In the **Cash Flow Forecast** field, select the forecast you have just created.

4. Specify the sources from which you want to take information out to do your cash flow prediction. For example, we have selected all of the available sources, as shown in the following screenshot:

5. Click on **OK**. The system will look on all the specified sources and will create lines on the **Cash Flow Worksheet**. On those lines, you will see: the **Source Type**, the **Source No.**, the **Cash Flow Date**, and the **Amount** in local currency.
6. You can modify the suggested lines, delete them, or create new ones. This will allow you to adjust the suggestion in order to have a better forecast.
7. Click on **Register**.

At this point, we have created our cash flow forecast and we have brought to it, all the information about incoming and outgoing cash movements. Now, it's time to analyze all this information to be able to detect any liquidity problems.

Open the cash flow forecast card and click on **CF Availability by Periods**. In this window, which is shown in the following screenshot, we can observe a liquidity problem in week 3. The liquidity problem will be solved in the fourth week. We can reschedule some of the purchase orders or negotiate a longer payment term with our vendors. Consider the following instance:

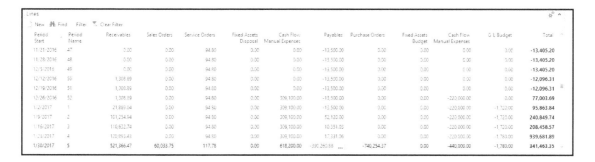

By double-clicking on the **Purchase Orders** value for week **3**, we will see which purchase orders are due this week. Actually, there is only one purchase order, which is due on 13/01/2017. We have talked to our vendor and have agreed to move the payment date to 21/01/2017. After updating the payment information on the purchase order, we have suggested and registered new lines for the forecast on the cash flow worksheet. As we can see on the **CF Availability by Periods** window now, the cash problem doesn't exist anymore.

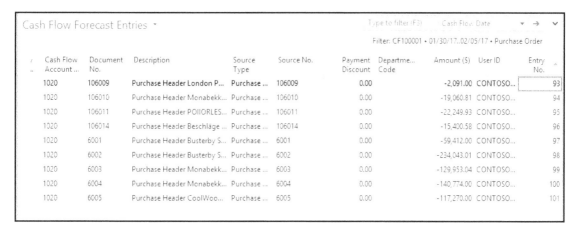

Creating manual expenses and revenues

Manual expenses and revenues can be created to complete the cash information that will be used to analyze the evolution of the company's liquidity. There is a lot of cash information that is already in the system (such as **Receivables** and **Payables**), but there is also a lot of other cash information that is not in the system and that we will have to input manually.

To create a cash flow manual expense, perform the following steps:

1. Navigate to **Departments | Financial Management | Cash Flow** and click on **Cash Flow Manual Expenses**.
2. Click on the **New** icon and create a new manual expense with the information shown in the following screenshot:

These are manual expenses such as **Personnel Costs**, **Running Costs**, and **Finance Costs** of **130000**, **75000**, **15000** for every month from **01/01/2017** to **12/31/2017**. For now, these expenses will be taken into account while suggesting worksheet lines for our forecasts.

Manual revenues are created in a similar way at **Departments | Financial Management | Cash Flow | Cash Flow Manual Revenues**.

Cash flow management setup

The cash flow management functionality uses its own chart of accounts: the chart of **Cash Flow Accounts**. You can define the chart of accounts you need. For those cash flow accounts that will get their information from the general ledger or from the budget, you will have to specify a G/L account filter and the type of G/L integration (balance, budget, or both):

No.	Name	Account Type	Totaling	Amount	G/L Accou...
0001	CashFlow	Begin-Total		0.00	
0002	Surplus	Begin-Total		0.00	
0009	Cash receipts	Begin-Total		0.00	
0010	Receivables	Entry		614,106.89	
0020	Open Sales Orders	Entry		524,236.43	
0030	Rentals	Entry		34,800.00	
0040	Financial Assets	Entry		74,400.00	
0050	Fixed Assets Disposals	Entry		0.00	
0060	Private Investments	Entry		3,600,000.00	
0070	Miscellaneous receipts	Entry		0.00	
0080	Open service orders	Entry		319.76	_____
0999	**Total of Cash Receipts**	End-Total	0009..0999	4,847,863.08	
1000	Cash disbursement	Begin-Total		0.00	
1010	Payables	Entry		-429,764.14	
1020	Open Purchase Orders	Entry		-740,254.37	
1030	Personnel costs	Entry		-1,560,000.00	
1040	Running costs	Entry		-900,000.00	
1050	Finance Costs	Entry		-180,000.00	

Once the chart of cash flow accounts is complete, we will have to complete the setup by navigating to **Departments** | **Financial Management** | **Cash Flow** | **Cash Flow Setup** and defining the **Cash Flow Account...** where the suggested lines will be posted from the different areas. In the following screenshot, you can see which information you will have to provide:

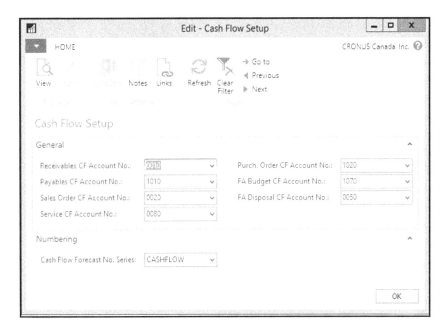

Summary

In this chapter, we saw the tools that can help companies in the task of predicting and anticipating financial events. You learned to create new budgets using different sources of information. You can manually introduce budgeted amounts, copy it from real general ledger entries with an adjustment factor, or import it from Excel. You also learned how to predict cash needs by analyzing several sources of information, such as liquid funds, receivables and payables, outstanding orders, and budgets.

So far, we have come across sales and purchases, bank account management, and different accounting processes. In Dynamics NAV, everything leads to accounting, but most of the operations inside the financial management area can be done with little accountancy knowledge. In the next chapter, we will learn the setup options that allow this to happen.

6

Financial Management Setup

In Dynamics NAV, everything leads to accounting, but as we have seen in the previous chapters, most operations inside the financial management area can be done with a little accountancy knowledge. In this chapter, we will learn the setup options that allow this to happen.

The topics that we will cover in this chapter are as follows:

- Posting groups
- Dimensions
- Number series
- The general setup

Understanding posting groups

Posting groups are the linking bridge between the G/L accounts and the accounts used on all application areas, such as items, customers, vendors, and fixed assets. Posting groups are used to notify the system which accounts to use on each transaction. There are three main types of posting group as follows:

- **Specific posting groups**: These are used to link subsidiary ledgers (namely the vendor ledger entries) to the general ledger. They are used to specify balance sheet accounts.
- **General posting groups**: Typically, these are used to specify income statement accounts that should be used on transactions. They are used to specify to whom and what we sell or buy.
- **TAX posting groups**: You use these to specify the tax rates, calculation types, and accounts.

Specific posting groups

Specific posting groups are mainly used to instruct the system about which balance sheet account to use for each subsidiary ledger. For example, the sum of balances of all customers must be equal to the balances of the accounts receivable in the balance sheet.

To avoid differences between general and subsidiary ledgers, balance accounts used on posting groups are usually set up to disallow direct posting.

In Dynamics NAV, you can find the following specific posting groups:

Posting Group name	Description
Customer Posting Groups	This specifies the accounts for transaction such as receivables, payment discounts, roundings, and interest and fees that relate to customers.
Vendor Posting Groups	This maps payable accounts, payment discount amounts, rounding accounts, and interest and fee accounts that relate to vendors.
Inventory Posting Group/Inventory Posting Setup	This maps inventory accounts, WIP accounts, and other accounts that relate to the inventory. Inventory posting groups define the type of inventory, while accounts are specified in the **Inventory Posting Setup** page in combination with locations.
Bank Account Posting Groups	This links a bank G/L account to a bank account.
Fixed asset posting groups	This specifies the accounts used in FA transactions such as posting its acquisition cost, or depreciation.
Job Posting Groups	This maps the accounts used in transactions involving jobs.

To access each posting group, type its name in the search box and select the corresponding link. The following screenshot shows the customer posting groups defined in the **CRONUS** International Ltd. demo company:

Code	Receivables Account	Service Charg...	Payment Disc. Deb...	Payment Disc. Cre...	Interest Account	Additional Fee Acco...	Add. Fee per Lin...	Invoice Roundin...	Debit Curr. Appln. R...	Credit Curr. Appln. Rn...	Debit Roundin...	Credit Roundin...	Payment Toleranc...	Payment Toleranc...
DOMESTIC	13100	45100	54800	80455	70200	70200		70400	70500	70500	70500	70500	80460	80470
EU	13200	45100	54800	80455	70200	70200		70400	70500	70500	70500	70500	80460	80470
FOREIGN	13200	45100	54800	80455	70200	70200		70400	70500	70500	70500	70500	80460	80470

As an example, when you post an invoice, a customer ledger is created and the account specified in the **Receivables Account** field is used to post the corresponding amount in the general ledger.

Specific posting groups are assigned to its corresponding cards in fields that have the same name. In **Customer Card**, for instance, you find a field called **Customer Posting Groups**, where you can assign one of the defined posting groups to each customer, in the same manner you find the **Bank Acc. Posting Group** field in the bank account card or the **FA Posting Group** field in the depreciation book lines of the FA card.

General posting groups

The main purpose of general posting groups is to bind subsidiary ledgers to income statement accounts. There are two different general posting groups, as follows:

- **General Business Posting Groups**: This specifies who we are selling to and who are we buying from. You need to specify them on Customers, Vendors, and, in some occasions, G/L accounts.

 G/L accounts require a business posting group if they are used in a transaction that requires VAT calculation.

- **General Product Posting Groups**: They specify what is being sold or purchased. They are assigned to **Items**, **Resources**, **G/L Accounts**, and **Item Charges**.

As a general rule, create as many business groups as needed to analyze sales by customers or purchases by vendors. Also, consider how many product groups are needed to analyze sales and purchases by products. As a rule, you create one general product posting group for each major product group reflected in the chart of accounts.

Navigate to **Departments** | **Administration** | **Application Setup** | **Financial Management** | **Posting Groups** to access both posting groups.

Take a look at the following screenshot:

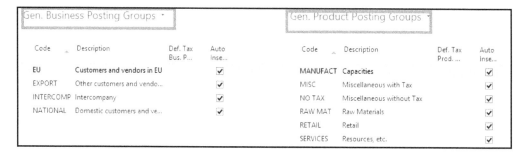

So far, we have defined groups, but we have not assigned them to G/L accounts. It is the mixture of a business and a product group that will define the account to be used. The following screenshot shows the general posting setup used in the **CRONUS** company:

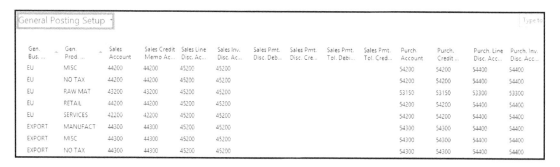

As an example, when you post an invoice with a customer in the **EXPORT** group and an item in the **MANUFACT** group, the account **6130** is used to post the corresponding amount in the general ledger, as specified in the **Sales Account** field.

Tax posting groups

Tax posting groups are used by the system to know how tax is to be calculated and posted, depending on who the item is sold to or purchased from and what is sold or purchased. Just like general posting groups, to define tax you need to create the following posting groups:

- Tax business posting groups that are assigned to customers and vendors
- Tax product posting groups that are assigned to items and resources
- Combinations of both are specified on the **TAX Posting Setup** page

In the earlier versions of Dynamics NAV 2016, the **TAX Posting Group** was known as the **VAT Posting Group**.

The following screenshot shows the **TAX Posting Setup** page for the export business group:

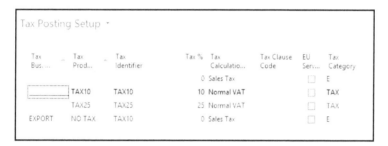

For each combination, you need to specify **TAX %**, **TAX Calculation Type**, and the general ledger accounts to use on sales and purchases. The accounts to use for unrealized VAT or to adjust VAT for payment discounts can be specified in additional fields.

You can select one of the following options for **TAX Calculation Type**:

- **Normal**: This option is used to calculate VAT.
- **Reverse charge**: This option is used when doing business with other countries in the EU where the purchaser must calculate and settle VAT accounts with the tax authorities.
- **Full VAT**: This option is used when the entire amount is considered VAT.
- **No taxable VAT**: When this option is selected, the system does not generate any VAT ledger entry. It is useful for concepts that are not subject to VAT.
- **Sales tax**: This option is used only if the program has to calculate US sales tax instead of VAT.

Setting up dimensions

In Chapter 4, *Reporting and Business Intelligence*, you learned about dimensions and how they can help to analyze the data registered into the system. To create dimensions and dimensions values, we perform the following steps:

1. Navigate to **Administration** | **Dimensions** and click on **New**.
2. Give the new dimension a code such as ITEM TYPE.
3. Click on **Dimension Values** and create the values shown in the following screenshot:

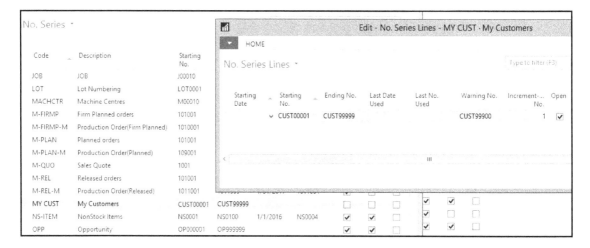

 You can create new dimension values on existing dimensions at any time.

Once the dimension is created, we have to tell the system whether it will be used as a global dimension or a shortcut dimension. This can be done in the **General Ledger Setup** window.

1. Navigate to **Departments** | **Financial Management** | **Setup** | **General Ledger Setup**.
2. In the **Dimensions** tab, select the **ITEM TYPE** dimension in the **Shortcut Dimension 7 code** field.

Change global dimensions
Once the global dimensions are assigned, you can change them using the **Change Global Dimensions** job found on the ribbon bar.

Number series

In Dynamics NAV, every document, transaction, or card (such as a customer or vendor card) must have a unique identification number by which it can be organized and tracked. To let the system help you with this, you can set up a number series performing the following steps:

1. Navigate to **Administration | Number Series**.
2. Click on **New**. Give the new number series a code, such as MY CUST, and a description, such as My Customers.
3. Check the **Default Nos.** field and the **Manual Nos.** field. This way, you can either use automatic or manual numbering with the number series.

If you need to check whether numbers are assigned chronologically, check the **Date Order** field.

4. Click on the **Lines** option from the ribbon bar and create the following line:

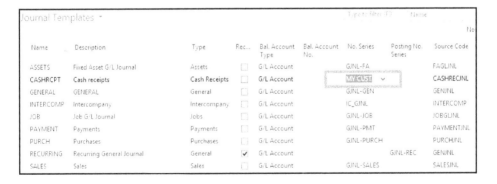

Name	Description	Type	Rec...	Bal. Account Type	Bal. Account No.	No. Series	Posting No. Series	Source Code
ASSETS	Fixed Asset G/L Journal	Assets	☐	G/L Account		GJNL-FA		FAGLJNL
CASHRCPT	Cash receipts	Cash Receipts	☐	G/L Account		MY CUST ∨		CASHRECJNL
GENERAL	GENERAL	General	☐	G/L Account		GJNL-GEN		GENJNL
INTERCOMP	Intercompany	Intercompany	☐	G/L Account		IC_GJNL		INTERCOMP
JOB	Job G/L Journal	Jobs	☐	G/L Account		GJNL-JOB		JOBGLJNL
PAYMENT	Payments	Payments	☐	G/L Account		GJNL-PMT		PAYMENTJNL
PURCH	Purchases	Purchases	☐	G/L Account		GJNL-PURCH		PURCHJNL
RECURRING	Recurring General Journal	General	✔	G/L Account			GJNL-REC	GENJNL
SALES	Sales	Sales	☐	G/L Account		GJNL-SALES		SALESJNL

If you need to use a new number every month or every year, create as many lines as needed, indicating the starting date on each of them.

5. To instruct the system to use these new number series when creating new customers, navigate to **Departments** | **Financial Management** | **Receivables** | **Setup** | **Sales & Receivables Setup**.

6. On the **Numbering** tab, select the **MY CUST** series in the **Customer Nos.** field.

7. Create a new customer to verify that the new series is being used.

Most setup pages contain a tab called **Numbering** where you can instruct the system about which series to use on each document, card, or transaction.

Number series can also be assigned to journal batches so that a correlative number is assigned every time you create or post new lines. The following screenshot shows the batches in the general journal. To assign a number when creating new journal lines, select a series in the **No. Series** field. If you select a series in the **Posting No. Series** option, the number will be assigned when posting the transaction, not when creating the line:

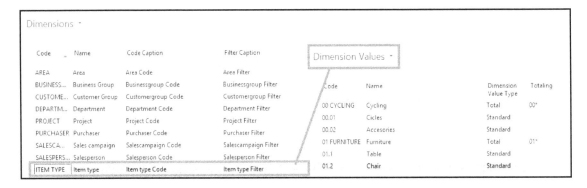

General setup

Every Dynamics NAV functional area has its own setup options that will determine the behavior of the application on that area. We will take a look at the setup of the functional areas we have seen in this book: General ledger, Sales, Purchases, and Inventory.

Most of the available setup options can be found via the following path: **Departments** | **Administration** | **Application Setup** | **Financial Management** | **Finance**, and you can choose among the different setups available.

The **General Ledger Setup** page is shown in the following screenshot:

The **General Ledger Setup** page allows you to determine general behaviors that will be used throughout the whole application. As an example, we have identified four setup groups, as follows:

- **Allowed posting dates**: We have explained the usage of this setup in `Chapter 3`, *Accounting Processes*.
- **Address format**: Different countries type address information in different orders. Here, you specify how addresses will be written on printed documents, such as invoices.
- **VAT setup**: With these options, you can determine different VAT calculation behaviors, such as rounding.

- **Payment tolerance**: If you have an invoice with an amount of **1001, 53** and you receive a payment of **1,000**, you may consider that the invoice has been paid. If you don't want that amount of **1, 53** to be pending forever, payment tolerance should be set up.

There are other setup options in the general ledger. On the **Dimensions** FastTab, the general dimensions are established, and on the **Numbering** FastTab, you specify which number series will be used for banks.

The **Sales & Receivables Setup** page and the **Purchases & Payables Setup** page are very similar and you can use them to specify the following:

- The numbering to be used for the master data (customer and vendors) and for the different documents
- How to post discounts to the general ledger, together with the invoice amount or separately to be able to see the discounts on the general ledger
- The default posting date and default quantities to post on documents
- Whether external document numbers are mandatory

The **Inventory Setup** page can be found by navigating to **Departments** | **Administration** | **Application Setup** | **Warehouse** | **Inventory** and can be used to specify the following:

- The numbering to be used for master data (items) and for different warehouse-specific documents
- Whether item costs should be automatically posted to the general ledger or not
- How to calculate an item's average cost

Summary

In this chapter, we saw what posting groups are and how they are used in the application to post multiple accounting transactions with no accounting knowledge needed. We have also seen other important setups such as the dimensions or the number series. All these configurations are vital for the application to work the way we want.

In the next chapter, we will see brief explanations of other areas that can be managed in Dynamics NAV regarding financial management.

7
Other Financial Functionalities

So far, we have covered the most important aspects of financial management with Dynamics NAV. But the application has a lot more possibilities regarding accounting and financial management. In this chapter, we will briefly explain all the other possibilities, which include the following topics:

- Currencies
- Intercompany postings
- Accounting implications of other areas
- XBRL
- E-services and document management

Currencies

Different countries use different currencies. The application can post transactions such as invoices or payments in different currencies and translate them into the **local currency** (**LCY**) according to the corresponding exchange rate.

Imagine that your local currency is Euro (EUR) and you sell your products or services to the United States of America, where the currency used is Dollar (USD).

You would first assign the USD currency to all those customers who do use this currency. You do so in the **Currency Code** field found in the **Foreign Trade** FastTab of the customer card.

Always leave the **Currency Code** field blank when using the local currency.

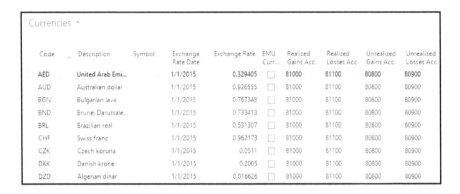

Then, you would inform the correct exchange rate by navigating to **Departments** | **Financial Management** | **Periodic Activities** | **Currency** | **Currencies**, selecting the appropriate currency, and clicking on **Exchange Rate**, as shown in the following screenshot:

Exchange rates have to be frequently updated in Dynamics NAV because they change constantly.

Now, if you prepare an invoice for this customer, you will see that the USD currency is used. This means that prices and amounts will be in dollars; however, you can always see the conversions to your local currency in all those fields that have the LCY acronym.

In the general ledger, amounts will always be shown on local currency. In other places, such as the posted invoice or the customer ledger entry, amounts will be shown both in local currency and in the used currency.

Currencies are available in the following application areas:

- Customers, vendors, and banks
- All transactions that can be done with a customer, a vendor, or a bank, such as invoices, payments, and so on
- Definition of item sales and purchase prices
- Definition of resources, sales prices, and so on

Intercompany postings

Intercompany postings are useful when you manage multiple companies at the same time and those companies do transactions between them (that is, a subsidiary company buys or sells products or services to another subsidiary company).

The intercompany functionality allows you to define the mapping between the items and chart of accounts of company A and the items and chart of accounts of company B. When company A wants to buy items from company B, company A creates a purchase order and then sends it electronically to company B. In company B, a sales order is automatically created with the appropriate items or G/L accounts. This way, the information is introduced only once and carried to the corresponding companies in the corresponding way.

Intercompany postings use a number of entries and documents for the relevant transactions:

- General journal entries
- Purchase and sales orders
- Purchase and sales invoices
- Credit memos
- Return orders

To set up Intercompany postings, the company must create a list of IC partners and an IC chart of accounts:

1. **Intercompany (IC) partners**: Set up customers and vendors as business partners and assign them IC partner codes. This permits exchange of IC purchase and sales documents, including items and item charges. You can do this by navigating to **Departments** | **Administration** | **Application Setup** | **Financial Management** | **Intercompany Postings** | **IC Partners**:

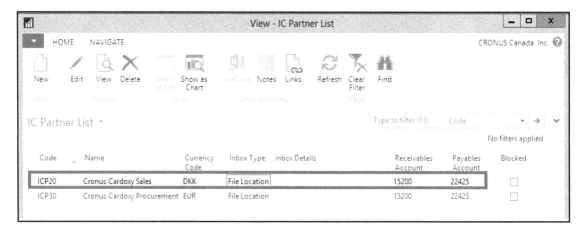

2. **IC chart of accounts**: Before IC partners can begin to transfer IC transactions electronically, each company must set up the IC chart of accounts in their company. You can do this by navigating to **Departments** | **Administration** | **Application Setup** | **Financial Management** | **Intercompany Postings** | **IC Chart of Accounts**:

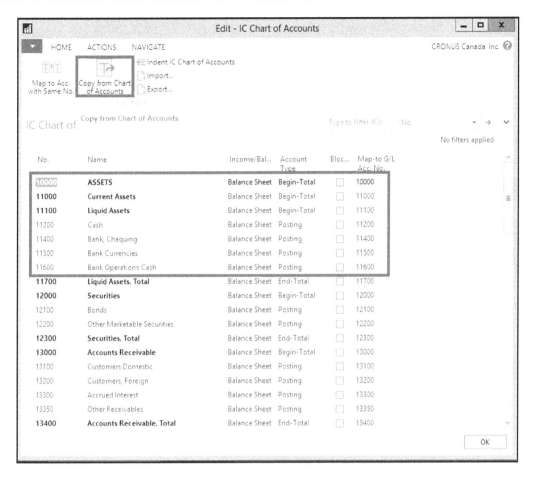

3. **IC journals**: These are used to post transactions with your intercompany partners. When you post an intercompany journal, a corresponding journal is created in your IC outbox that you can transfer to your partner. Your partner can then post the journal in their company, without having to re-enter the data:

   1. In the search box, enter `IC General Journal`, and/or you can navigate to **Departments** | **Financial Management** | **General Ledger** | **IC General Journal**.

2. Enter the details as follows:

- In the **Account Type** field, select **IC Partner**. In the **Account No.** field, select the IC partner code that you will send the transaction to.
- In the **IC Partner G/L Acc. No.** field, enter the IC general ledger account that the amount will be posted to in your partner's company.
- After filling in the fields, post the journal.

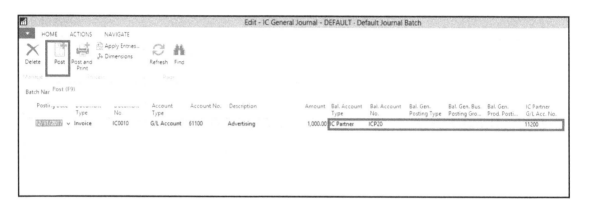

Accounting implications of other areas

In this book, we saw the financial management of Dynamics NAV and also the accounting implication the sales and the purchase areas have. Other functional areas such as jobs, service, warehouse, or manufacturing also have some kind of accounting implications that will be briefly explained in this section.

Jobs

The Job functional area is meant to manage projects and perform tasks such as configuring the job, scheduling resources, monitor progress, and so on.

This area has two kinds of accounting implications, which are as follows:

- It can create sales invoices. The accounting implication of those sales invoices are the same as regular sales invoices.

- **Work in Process** (**WIP**) can be calculated and posted to the general ledger. Multiple WIP methods can be configured to calculate WIP for a specific job.

Service

The Service functional area is meant to manage post-sale services and maintain a record of customers.

Within this area, service invoices can be created and posted, which will end up in postings to the general ledger and in customer ledger entries that will have to be paid later on.

Warehouse

The Warehouse functional area is meant to manage all warehouse-related processes, such as receiving items from vendors, stocking them into the warehouse, picking and sending items to customers and perform the necessary internal item movements.

This area is all about items. Items have a cost that has to be posted to the general ledger in order to be able to know our inventory valuation. We have already talked about inventory valuation earlier on this book.

Manufacturing

The Manufacturing functional area is meant to manage and plan the transformation of inputs into finished goods.

This area has two kinds of accounting implications:

- It works with items, which have a cost that has to be posted to the general ledger in order to be able to know our inventory valuation. We have already talked about inventory valuation earlier on this book.
- WIP can be calculated and posted to the general ledger.

XBRL

eXtensible Business Reporting Language (**XBRL**) is a global standard for exchanging business information such as financial statements or other such information. Dynamics NAV can export financial data using the XBRL standard.

The idea is that someone who wants to get financial information from you would provide you a taxonomy (an XML document), which would contain one or more schemas with lines you should fill out. You would import this taxonomy into the program and fill out the schema or schemas by entering the account or accounts that correspond to each line in the schema and other required information. Once it is filled out, export it from the application and send it to the requester.

E-services and document management

Microsoft dynamics NAV 2016 allows you to capture and store invoices and credit memos as incoming documents and use them to create corresponding purchase documents or journal lines. As an alternative to e-mailing as file attachments, you can send and receive documents electronically. By electronic document, we mean a standard-compliant file representing a business document, such as an invoice from a vendor that you can receive and convert to a purchase invoice in Microsoft Dynamics NAV. The exchange of electronic documents between two trading partners is performed by an external provider of document exchange services.

Document exchange service

The Microsoft Dynamics NAV 2016 version supports sending and receiving electronic invoices and credit memos in the PEPPOL format, which is supported by the largest providers of document exchange services. A major provider of document exchange services is preconfigured and ready to be set up for your company. You can perform the Document Exchange Service setup by navigating to **Departments** | **Administration** | **IT Administration** | **Services** | **Document Exchange Service setup**:

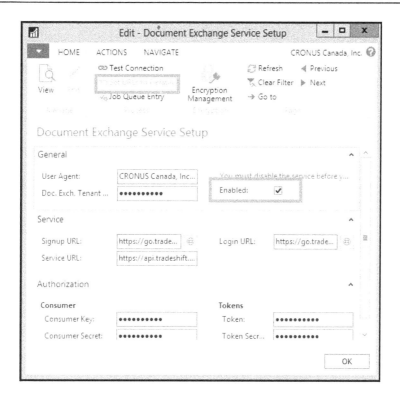

Once you enable the `Document Exchange Service` setup, these **Job Queue** entries will be auto-created:

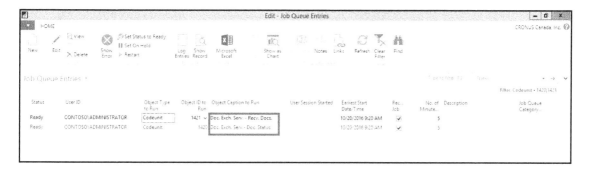

The OCR service

From PDF or image files representing incoming documents, you can have an external **Optical Character Recognition (OCR)** service to create electronic documents that you can then convert to document records in Microsoft Dynamics NAV, like for electronic PEPPOL documents. For example, when you receive an invoice in the PDF format from your vendor, you can send it to the OCR service from the **Incoming Documents** window. After a few seconds, you will receive the file back as an electronic invoice that can be converted to a purchase invoice for the vendor. If you send the file to the OCR service by e-mail, then a new incoming document record is automatically created when you receive the electronic document back.

Then, you can set up the OCR service by navigating to **Departments** | **Administration** | **IT Administration** | **Services** | **OCR Service setup**:

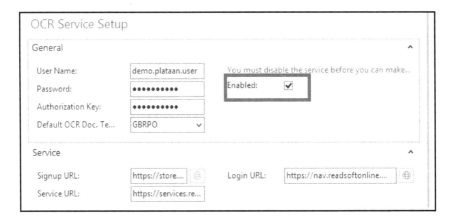

Once you enable the OCR setup, these **Job Queue** entries will be auto-created:

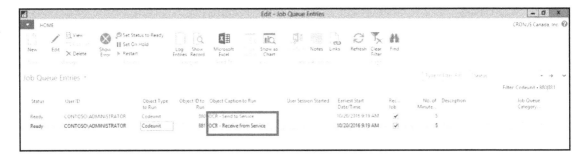

Simple Mail Transfer Protocol (SMTP)

You can send attachments by e-mail from Microsoft Dynamics NAV. The default e-mail sender address is based on the settings in the **SMTP Mail Setup** window. If SMTP is not configured or Outlook is not available, the .pdf file will open instead.

Then, you can perform the SMTP Mail setup by navigating to **Departments** | **Administration** | **IT Administration** | **Services** | **SMTP Mail setup**:

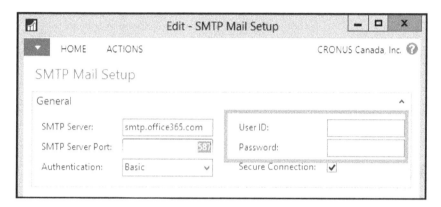

Process

We can test the whole process in **Sales Invoice** and send it electronically. For this, check the following steps:

1. Create the sales invoice by navigating to **Departments** | **Sales Marketing** | **Sales Invoice**.
2. Select **10000** as the customer number.
3. Select the **Bicycle** item in the **Lines** area with the quantity **1**.

4. Action pane, click on **Post** and send it as follows:

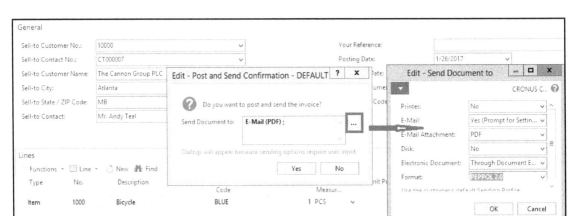

Summary

In this chapter, you learned about other possibilities of the financial management area of Dynamics NAV, such as the use of multiple currencies, intercompany postings, the accounting implications of other areas, the XBRL standard for reporting business information, document exchange by PEPPOL, and LCS.

In the next chapter, we will work on fixed assets, where we will see the complete life cycle of fixed asset from acquisition to disposal, maintenance expenses, budgeted asset, and how to insure fixed assets in NAV 2016.

8

Fixed Asset Setup and Transactions

This book is almost over. We have covered the most important aspects of financial management with Dynamics NAV. But, in this chapter, you will learn about the complete life cycle of a Fixed Asset from acquisition to disposal. In this chapter, we will do the following:

- Fixed Asset setup
- Fixed Asset posting
- Fixed Asset reporting

What are fixed assets?

The Fixed Asset functionality in Microsoft Dynamics NAV provides an overview of your fixed assets and ensures correct periodic depreciation. It also enable you to keep track of your maintenance costs, manage insurance policies related to fixed assets, post fixed asset transactions, and generate various reports and statistics.

The following is the fixed asset process flow:

1. **Fixed Assets setup**: For each fixed asset, you must set up a card containing information about the asset, such as a depreciation book, depreciation method, fixed asset posting group, maintenance information, and so on.
2. **Depreciation**: You can set up multiple depreciation books to accommodate various kinds of depreciation. You can calculate either manual or automatic depreciation.

3. **Posting transactions**: All posting in the Fixed Assets application area is done from journals. There are four different journals:
   - The FA G/L journal
   - The FA journal
   - The FA reclassification journal
   - The insurance journal

4. **Maintenance**: For each asset, you can record maintenance costs and the next service date. Keeping track of maintenance expenses can be important for budgeting purposes and for making decisions about whether to replace a fixed asset.

5. **Insurance**: Each fixed asset can be attached to one or more insurance policies. You can, therefore, easily verify that insurance policy amounts are in accordance with the value of the assets that are linked to the policy. This also makes it easy to monitor annual insurance premiums.

6. **Statistics and reports**: For each fixed asset depreciation book, there is a statistics window that provides a quick overview of the book value, depreciable basis, accumulated depreciation, and gains or losses on sales. Each main asset has its own statistics window.

There are several standard reports available and some of these can be tailored to meet specific needs.

The Fixed Asset cards

We specify information about fixed assets, such as the serial number, responsible employee, posting codes, and maintenance information. There is one card for each fixed asset. Each card contains several FastTabs with different types of information about the fixed asset.

To access the **FA Card**, navigate to **Departments** ∣ **Financial Management** ∣ **Fixed Asset** ∣ **Fixed Asset**. Then, create a **New Fixed Asset** as shown in the following screenshot:

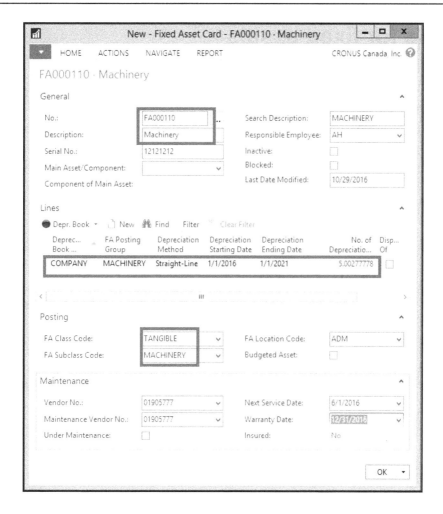

Fixed Asset transactions

All **Fixed Asset** (**FA**) transactions must be posted in a fixed assets journal. If a fixed asset is connected to a depreciation book integrated with the general ledger, the FA G/L journal is used.

Basic transactions for fixed assets are depreciations, acquisition costs, write-downs, and disposals. You can correct entries that have already been posted if an amount changes for some reason or if errors exist in posted transactions. You can also create reports, budgets, cost-accounting, and indexation for fixed assets.

Journals for fixed assets

All fixed asset transactions can be posted through the following four journals:

- **FA G/L journal**: All entries in this journal will be posted to both the fixed asset ledger and the general ledger as per the fixed asset posting group
- **FA journal**: All entries posted in this journal are posted only to the fixed asset ledger
- **FA reclassification journal**: All entries posted in this journal are used to transfer, split, or combine fixed assets
- **Insurance journal**: All entries posted in this journal are used to post insurance coverage ledger entries

Acquiring fixed assets

You can acquire a fixed asset by using FA G/L journal, purchase order, purchase invoice, or FA journal without affecting G/L.

It is common practice to enter the salvage value together with the purchase. You can only fill in the **Salvage Value** field if you have selected the **Acquisition Cost** option in the **FA Posting Type** field. In this case, enter the salvage value for the fixed asset in the field.

Typically, the salvage value must be entered as a negative amount.

Purchasing fixed assets

Before purchasing a fixed asset, you must set up a fixed asset using the fixed asset card (as shown in the previous screenshot).

To purchase a fixed asset and post the acquisition costs, follow these steps:

1. In the navigation pane, go to **Departments** | **Financial Management** | **Payables** | **Purchase Invoices**.
2. Click on **New**.
3. In the **Buy-from Vendor No.** field, click on the field and select vendor **44127904**.
4. In the **Vendor Invoice No.** field, enter 2016-E-101.
5. In the **Lines** FastTab, right-click on the header and use the **Choose Columns** function to add the **FA Posting Type** field.
6. In the **Type** field, select **Fixed Asset**.

7. In the **No.** field, select **FA000110**.
8. In the **Quantity** field, enter 1.
9. In the **Direct Unit Cost Excl. VAT** field, enter 11,000.00.
10. In the **FA Posting Type** field, select **Acquisition Cost**
11. Click on **Post** to post the purchase of the **Fixed Asset**.
12. When you receive the message **Do you want to post the Invoice?**, click on **Yes**.

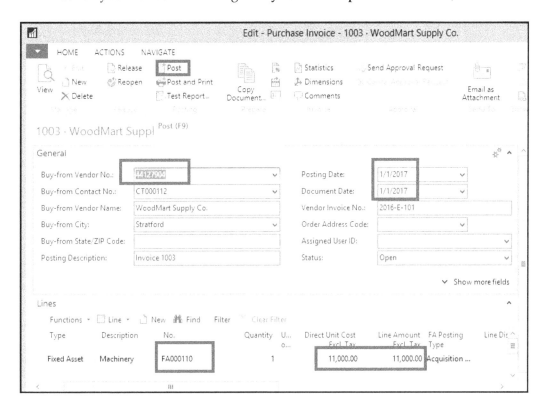

Calculating and posting depreciation

Depreciation is used to allocate fixed assets over their depreciable life. Fixed asset depreciation can be calculated and posted using two methods:

- **Manual**: We can use the FA G/L journal or the FA journal
- **Automatic**: We can run the Calculate Depreciation batch job

Manual depreciation with the FA G/L Journal

To manually post depreciation for a fixed asset that has integration with the general ledger, use the FA G/L journal:

1. In the navigation pane, go to **Departments** | **Financial Management** | **Fixed Assets** | **FA G/L Journals**.
2. In the **FA G/L Journal** window, in the **Posting Date** field, enter the relevant posting date.
3. In the **Account Type** field, click on the field and then select **Fixed Asset**.
4. In the **Account No.** field, click on the field and then select the fixed asset for which you want to post the depreciation.
5. In the **Depreciation Book Code** field, click on the field and then select the depreciation book associated with the selected fixed asset and integrated with the general ledger, for example, COMPANY.
6. In the **FA Posting Type** field, click on the field and then select **Depreciation**.
7. Make sure that an allocation key is set up in the FA posting group and then click on **Insert FA Bal. Account.** in the **Home** FastTab. Balancing lines with different department codes are now created automatically. You can use the **Choose Columns** function to add the **Department Code** field.
8. Click on **Post** to post the depreciation.
9. When you receive the message **Do you want to post the journal lines?**, click on **Yes**.
10. When you receive the message **The journal lines were successfully posted.**, click on **OK**.

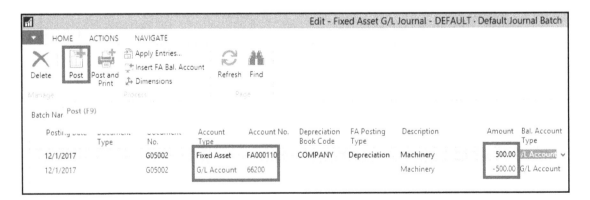

Calculating depreciation automatically

Calculate Depreciation is a batch job that automatically calculates depreciation based on the conditions that you set up on the batch job request page. Sold, blocked, or inactive assets, and assets that use the manual depreciation method are excluded from the automatic depreciation calculation. The batch job automatically creates journal lines, and you only have to check and post the created journal lines in the FA G/L journal.

The following demonstration explains how to calculate depreciation for the fixed asset **FA000110** using the **Calculate Depreciation** batch job.

To calculate depreciation, follow these steps:

1. In the navigation pane, go to **Departments** | **Financial Management** | **Fixed Assets** | **Fixed Assets**.
2. In the **Fixed Assets** window, select the line with fixed asset **FA000110**, and then click on **Ledger Entries** in the **Navigate** FastTab. The new depreciation must be calculated for January.
3. Close the **FA Ledger Entries** window.
4. Double-click on **FA000110**. Next, in the **Actions** FastTab in the **General** group, click on **Calculate Depreciation**. The **Calculate Depreciation** batch job request page will appear.
5. In the **Options** FastTab, in the **Depreciation Book** field, select **COMPANY**.
6. In the **FA Posting Date** field, type 1/1/2017.
7. Select the **Insert Bal. Account** checkbox.

8. In the **Fixed Asset** FastTab, set the filter for the **No.** field to **FA000110**:

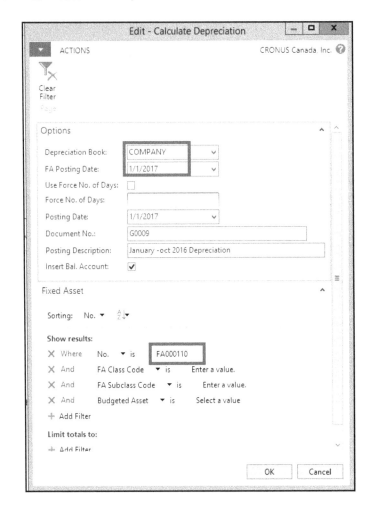

9. Click on **OK** to calculate the depreciation on January 1, 2017. The batch job calculates the depreciation for the fixed asset number **FA000110** and creates the lines in the Fixed Asset G/L journal.

10. Close the fixed assets card.

11. Navigate to **Departments** | **Financial Management** | **Fixed Assets** | **FA G/L Journals**.

12. The **Fixed Asset G/L Journal** window contains the lines created by the **Calculate Depreciation** batch job.

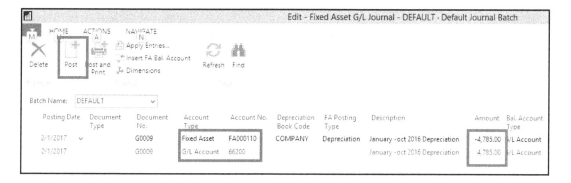

13. View the lines and then click on **Post** to post the depreciation.

14. When you receive the message **Do you want to post the journal lines?**, click on **Yes**.

15. When you receive the message **The journal lines were successfully posted.**, click on **OK**.

16. Click on **OK** to close the **Fixed Asset G/L Journal** window.

Write-down and appreciation of fixed assets

- Let's take a look at what write-down and appreciation mean. A write-down is a decrease in the value of a fixed asset. A decrease may be the result of the asset becoming out-of-date or damaged

- An appreciation is an increase in the value of a fixed asset (typically, land and buildings). It can also be used for a fixed asset that increases in value because of increased demand for the item.

Fixed Asset disposals

Disposal of the whole or a part of a fixed asset is the last step in the typical life cycle of a fixed asset. For partially disposed of fixed assets, you can post several disposal entries. Before you can dispose of parts of an asset, you must split the asset into two separate assets, as follows:

- Use the **FA G/L journal** to post a disposal transaction to a depreciation book for which the disposal has a general ledger integration

- Use the **FA journal** to post a disposal transaction to a depreciation book for which the disposal does not have a general ledger integration

Set up the disposal method for each depreciation book in the **Disposal Calculation Method** field. The program can handle disposals using one of the following methods:

- **Net method**: Post to either a disposal loss or gain account. This is the most common disposal method.
- **Gross method**: Post to a book value gain or loss account and to a sales gain or loss account. When you enter the sales price in a journal, the program calculates the gain or loss on the disposal and calculates all other relevant entries. The gain or loss amount is calculated automatically from the difference between the sales price and the book value.

Posting the disposal through the FA G/L Journal

To post disposals through the FA G/L journal, follow these steps:

1. In the navigation pane, go to **Financial Management | Fixed Assets | FA G/L Journals**.
2. In the **Fixed Asset G/L Journal** window, enter the appropriate information on the line.
3. In the **Amount** field, enter the disposal amount as a credit or negative number.
4. In the **Actions** FastTab, click on **Post**.
5. When you receive the message **Do you want to post the journal lines?**, click on **Yes**.
6. When you receive the message **The journal lines were successfully posted.**, click on **OK**.

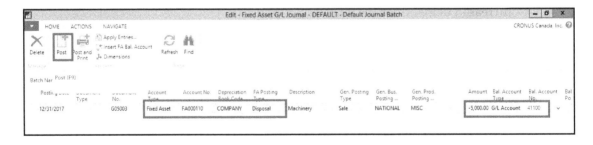

Budget Fixed Asset transactions

When you set up a budgeted asset, you can plan for the addition of assets. After an asset is bought, you must create the new asset and post it with the actual acquisition cost through the FA journal, a purchase invoice, or the FA G/L journal. You can then compare the budgeted cost to the actual cost. A budgeted asset is not integrated to the general ledger. This information is available from the FA projected value report.

You can indicate that the asset was created for budgeting by selecting the **Budgeted Asset** checkbox on the fixed asset card in the **Posting** FastTab.

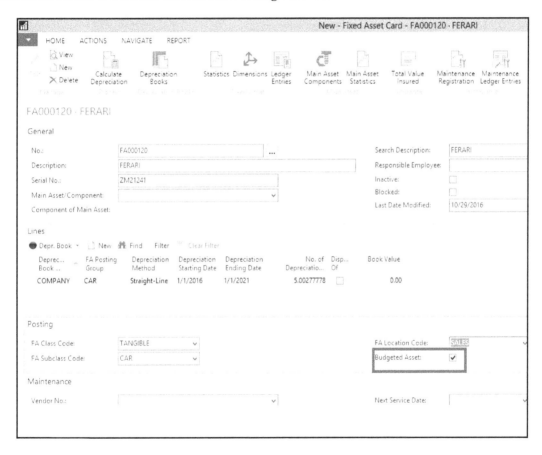

Demonstration – Budget for future acquisition costs

In this demonstration, we will prepare a budget for future acquisition costs by setting up a fixed asset card for fixed assets that the company intends to buy in the future.

To budget for future acquisition costs, follow these steps:

1. Navigate to **Departments** | **Financial Management** | **Fixed Assets (Group)** | **Fixed Assets (List Page)**.
2. Click on **New** to create a new fixed asset.
3. Press *Enter* to automatically assign a number to the asset.
4. In the **Description** field, type `Ferrari`.
5. In the **Serial No.** field, type `ZM 21 241`.
6. In the **Lines** FastTab in the **Depreciation Book Code** field, click on the field and then select **COMPANY**.
7. In the **FA Posting Group** field, click on the field and select **CAR**.
8. In the **Depreciation Method** field, click on the field and select **Straight-line**.
9. In the **Depreciation Starting Date** field, type `1/1/2016`.
10. In the **Depreciation Ending Date** field, type `1/31/2021`.
11. In the **Posting** FastTab in the **FA Class Code** field, click on the field and select **TANGIBLE**.
12. In the **FA Subclass Code** field, click on the field and select **CAR**.
13. In the **FA Location Code** field, click on the field and select **SALES**.
14. Select the **Budgeted Asset** checkbox to prevent posting to the general ledger

15. Close the **Fixed Asset Card** window.
16. Navigate to **Departments** | **Financial Management** | **Fixed Assets** | **FA Journals** to open the **Fixed Asset Journal** window.
17. Enter and post the budgeted acquisition cost as shown in the following screenshot and then post the line:

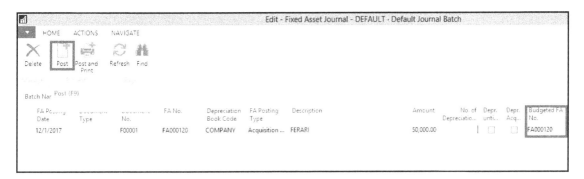

Reclassifiying assets

You can use asset transfers when you want to transfer, split, or combine assets.

Use the reclassification journal for all postings from asset transfers.

Transferring assets

When you transfer a fixed asset, the program moves the fixed asset entries (acquisition cost and depreciation) from one fixed asset account to another fixed asset account. To understand this, let's take a look at the following demonstration:

1. Create a new Fixed Asset:

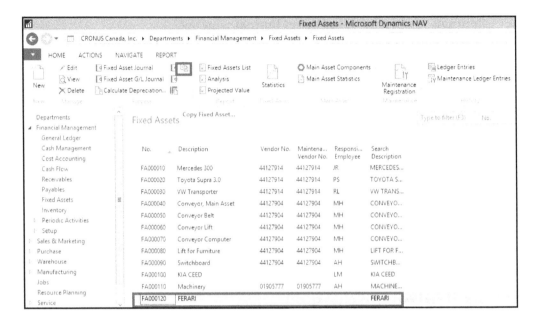

2. Copy from the existing Fixed Asset:

3. View the new Asset:

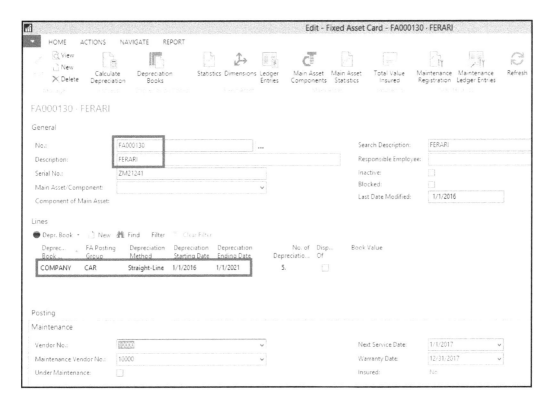

4. Acquire the new asset from the FA G/L journal:

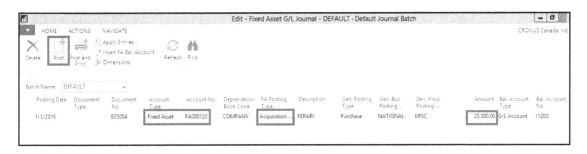

5. Split the new Fixed Asset (reclassify the FA by 50% by transferring value to another FA):

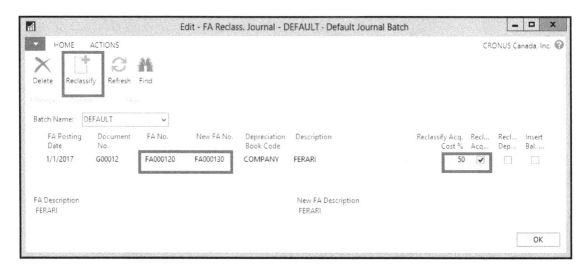

6. Post the reclassification:

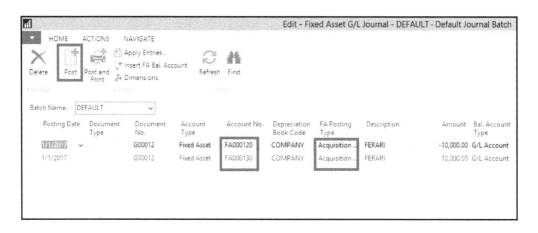

Setting up maintenance information

Maintenance expenses are routine periodic costs charged to preserve the value of fixed assets. Unlike capital improvements, maintenance expenses do not increase the value of the assets.

To use the fixed asset maintenance functionality in Microsoft Dynamics, you should set up the following:

1. Maintenance information on the Fixed Asset card:

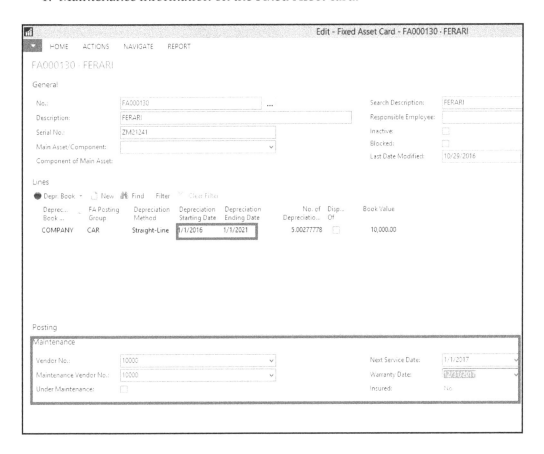

2. Fixed Asset posting groups to allow posting of the maintenance costs to the general ledger:

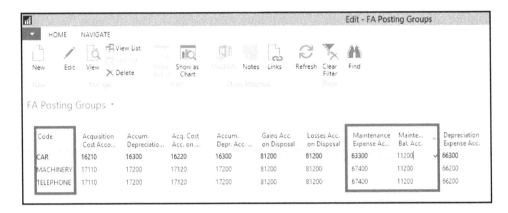

3. Maintenance code so that you can select the type of maintenance when you post maintenance costs:

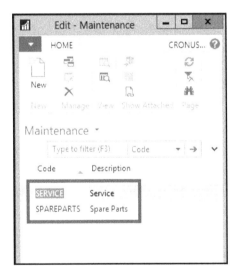

Maintenance registration and costs

Every time a fixed asset is sent for service, you have to record the relevant information, such as the date of service, vendor number, service agent name, and phone number.

When the service is completed and you receive a maintenance invoice, you register the maintenance costs through an FA G/L journal, purchase invoice, or FA journal, depending on whether the associated depreciation book is integrated with the general ledger.

Keeping track of service visits

Every time someone performs maintenance on a fixed asset, you can register this in the **Maintenance Registration** window.

To track a service visit, follow these steps:

1. In the navigation pane, go to **Departments** | **Financial Management** | **Fixed Assets** | **Fixed Assets**.
2. Select the line with the fixed asset for which you want to register a service visit.
3. In the **Home** FastTab, click on **Maintenance Registration**:

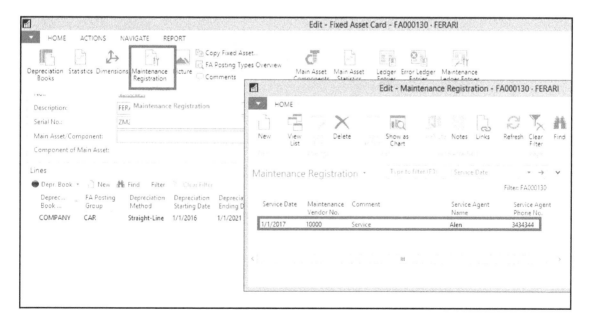

Recording maintenance costs

When you receive the maintenance invoice, you can record the maintenance costs in Microsoft Dynamics NAV 2016 in one of the following ways:

- If G/L integration is activated for the depreciation book, use a purchase invoice or an FA G/L journal:

- If G/L integration is not activated for the depreciation book, use only an FA journal:

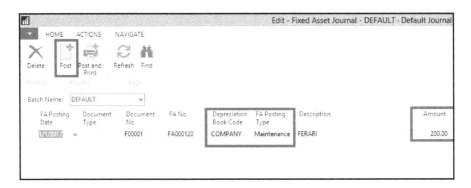

Setting up insurance information

You should set up general information about an insurance policy on the insurance card. You can create one insurance card for each insurance policy.

The Fixed Asset Setup page

In the **Fixed Assets Setup** window, you set up general information about your fixed asset insurance.

To set up general information about a fixed asset insurance, go to **Departments** | **Financial Management** | **Fixed Assets** | **FA Setup**.

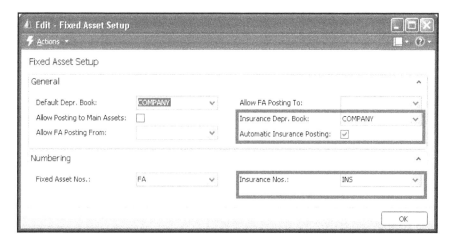

Insurance types

In Microsoft Dynamics NAV 2016, you can group insurance policies into insurance types, for example, theft or fire insurance.

To set up the insurance types, go to **Departments** | **Financial Management** | **Fixed Assets** | **Insurance Types**.

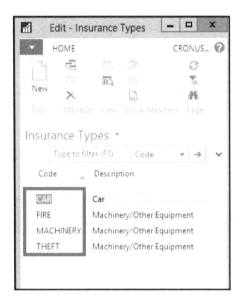

Insurance card

You should create an insurance card for each insurance policy related to fixed assets. On the insurance card, you specify general information about the insurance policy:

1. To set up a new insurance policy, in the navigation pane go to **Departments** | **Financial Management**|**Fixed Assets** | **Insurance**.
2. Click on **New** to create a new insurance card.
3. In the **General** FastTab, fill in the fields shown in the following table. Click on the **No.** field and press *Enter*:

Field	Value
No.	Auto
Description	Car Insurance
Effective Date	01/01/16
Insurance Type	CAR
Policy No.	443434343444

Annual Premium	500.00
Policy Coverage	20,000.00

The following will appear in the window:

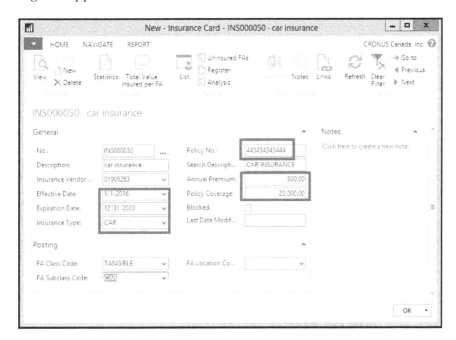

Attaching assets to insurance policies

In Microsoft Dynamics NAV 2016, you can attach any asset to an insurance policy. Attaching fixed assets to insurance policies gives you an easy way to find the relevant insurance policy for an asset when you want it.

Linking fixed assets to insurance policies

After you finish setting up the insurance information, the fixed assets can be linked to the insurance policies.

You can link one or more assets to a single insurance policy. You can also link one asset to the same insurance policy with different amounts.

A fixed asset can be attached to an insurance policy in one of the following two ways:

- Post an acquisition cost with the **Insurance No.** field filled in on the FA journal, the FA G/L journal line, or on the purchase invoice
- Post an acquisition cost without filling in the **Insurance No.** field on the journal line and then use the insurance journal to post the acquisition cost to the insurance coverage ledger

You can post the acquisition cost to the insurance coverage ledger from any of the following:

- Purchase invoice
- Insurance journal
- FA G/L journal
- FA journal

When the **Insurance No.** field has a value, the **Insured** field in the **Maintenance** FastTab in the **Fixed Asset Card** window is automatically set to **Yes**.

After you sell a fixed asset, the program automatically sets the **Insured** field on the fixed asset card to **No**.

Linking a fixed asset to an insurance policy through an insurance journal

If you posted the acquisition cost of a fixed asset without linking it to an insurance policy, either from the purchase invoice or from one of the FA journals, you can link the fixed asset to an insurance policy by posting the acquisition cost from an insurance journal.

For example, if you did not enter insurance number INS000040 in the **Insurance No.** field on the purchase invoice for Fixed Asset FA1500, you can still attach the insurance policy to the asset's acquisition cost from an insurance journal.

To post an insurance journal, follow these steps:

1. In the navigation pane, go to **Departments | Financial Management | Fixed Assets | Insurance Journals**.
2. In the **Posting Date** field, type 1/1/2016.
3. In the **Insurance No.** field, enter INS000050.
4. In the **FA No.** field, enter FA00120.

5. In the **Amount** field, type 200000.00.

6. In the **Amount** field in the journal line, enter the acquisition cost of the asset. For this example, use the previous example's information for FA00120. Enter FA00120 in the **FA No.** field, enter INS000050 in the Insurance No. field, and enter the acquisition cost as 20000.00 in the **Amount** field.

7. Click on **Post** to post the journal.

8. When you receive the message **Do you want to post the journal lines?**, click on **Yes**.

9. When you receive the message **The journal lines were successfully posted.**, click **OK**.

10. In the navigation pane, go to **Departments | Financial Management | Fixed Assets | Fixed Assets** and then double-click on the line with the fixed asset FA00120 to open the fixed asset card.

11. To verify the total value insured for the fixed asset, click on **Total Value Insured** in the **Navigate** FastTab.

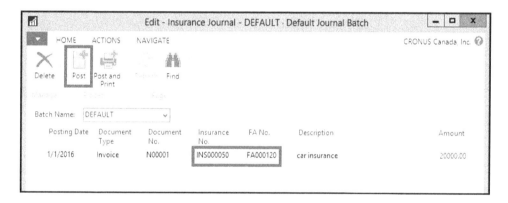

Fixed Asset reports

We have several standard reports in NAV 2016 for general ledgers, fixed assets, maintenance, insurance, depreciation, book value, and so on. But here we will discuss only a few of them.

Maintenance details report

This report shows detailed maintenance expenses for fixed assets. The report can show maintenance expenses for fixed assets for different time periods, broken down by maintenance types or other categories such as, fixed asset class.

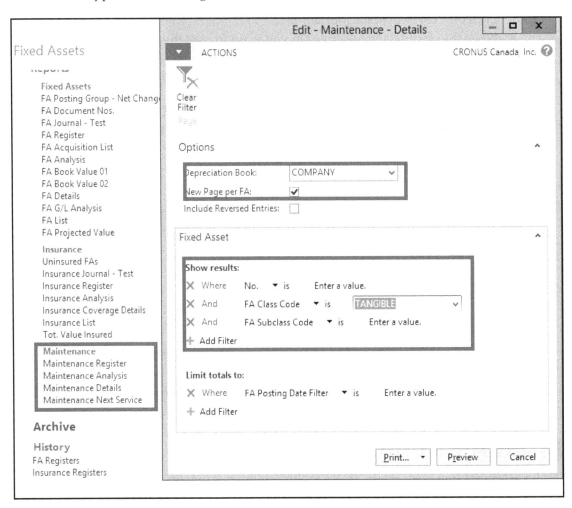

Insurance coverage details report

Insurance coverage details report prints the insurance–the **Total Value Insured** report. It shows which insurance policies cover each asset and specifies the amount.

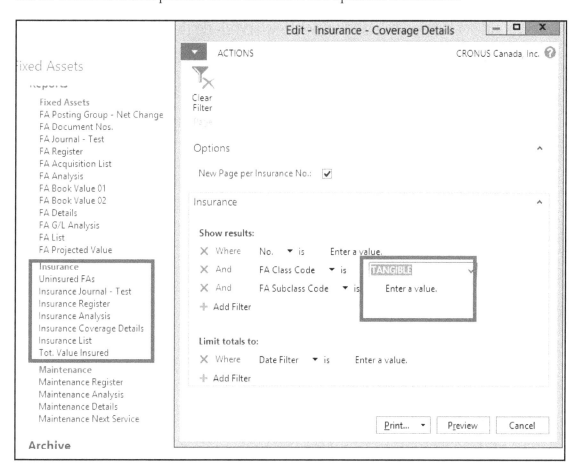

Fixed Asset details report

This report shows an analysis of your FA with various types of data for individual assets and/or groups of assets. In the **Fixed Assets** FastTab, you can set filters if you want the report to include only certain fixed assets. In the **Options** FastTab, you can choose from a number of options to tailor the report to meet your specific needs:

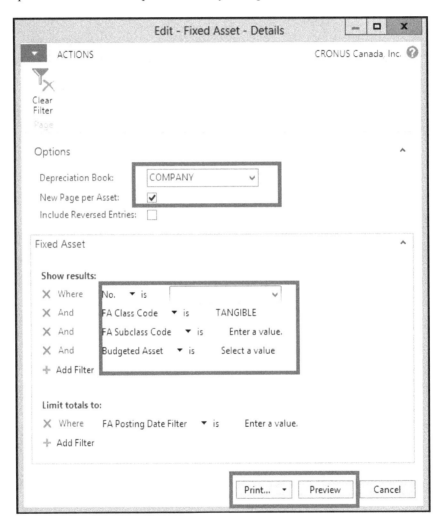

FA register report

This report shows details of transactions, which includes the journal type, date, user ID, batch, and so on, for all fixed assets.

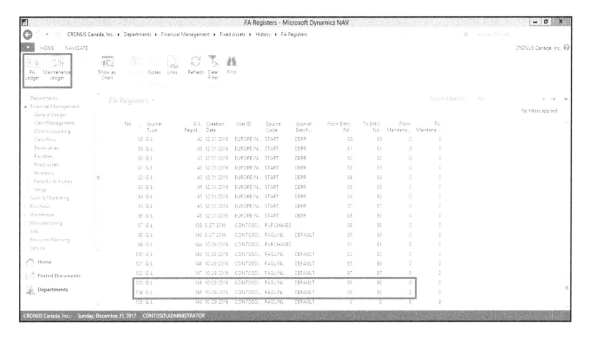

Microsoft announces Dynamics® 365 at WPC

In Microsoft's **World Partner Conference** (**WPC**), Microsoft released project Madeira, a new platform that looks a little bit like a simplified mix of Office 365 and the basic modules of Microsoft Dynamics® NAV. Although this is something that is an exciting prospect, one of the big issues that people have had in general is understanding the difference between all of the Dynamics products. Let's take a look.

What is Microsoft Dynamics 365?

Microsoft Dynamics 365 is an online-only business software solution. This is made up of two offerings:

- **Dynamics 365 Business Edition**: This is **Project Madeira** (essentially Dynamics NAV and Office 365 fully integrated), aimed at small businesses that need a limited and off-the-shelf solution.
  Project Madeira is the code name for a new cloud offering hosted by Microsoft inside Office 365. The solution is based on Microsoft Dynamics NAV. Some of its features are as follows:
    - Madeira was originally the code name for the next version of Dynamics NAV.
    - Microsoft has been working on making Dynamics NAV, a first class citizen on Azure, and in Office 365. With NAV 2015 and 2016, companies can already connect their on-premise ERP solution to Azure Active Directory and their Office 365 account and run a hybrid cloud/on-premise solution.
    - This works really well for midsize and larger organizations.
    - Madeira Microsoft is now taking this one step further by hosting the solution themselves and making the onboarding very easy.
- **Dynamics 365 Enterprise Edition**: This is something new based on Dynamics AX, CRM online, and Office 365, again fully integrated.

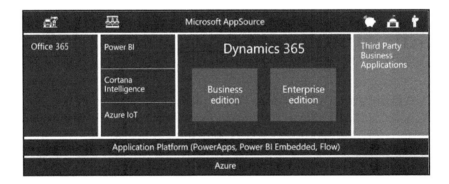

Dynamics 365 is not a replacement for the existing Dynamics products. In fact, Microsoft has made it quite clear that Dynamics NAV will continue to be developed, and a lot of the new tools and functionality will be available across packages.

The following screenshot provides the difference between the two. The **Business edition** provides the **Financials** choice apart from **Sales** and **Marketing,** whereas **Enterprise edition** provides the latter and some more functionality:

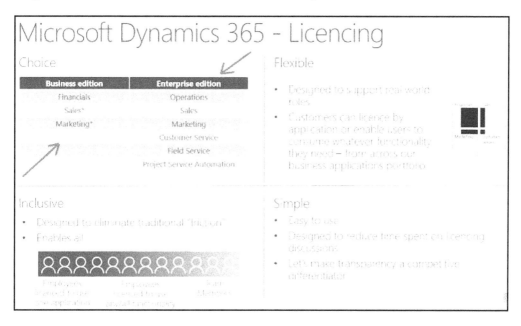

Summary

In this chapter, you learned about other financial management possibilities in Dynamics NAV, such as the use of fixed assets and ensuring correct periodic depreciation. You also learned to keep track of your depreciation, maintenance costs, insurance policies, and lending assets related to fixed assets; post fixed asset transactions; and generate various reports and statistics. You're now familiar with the complete life cycle of a Fixed Asset from acquisition to disposal.

In the previous chapters, we discussed all other financial concepts (from basic to advanced) such as configuring G/L account card, currency, posting groups, multiple transactions, cash and bank management, and the complete P2P and O2C cycle. You are now ready to start using Microsoft Dynamics NAV 2016 to implement financial management in your company.

Index

A

account schedules
  using 123, 124
accountancy 10
accounting implications
  of areas 160
  of Job functional area 160
  of Manufacturing functional area 161
  of Service functional area 161
  of Warehouse functional area 161
accounting periods
  closing 98, 99
accounting transactions
  posting 75
  recurring journals 78
  standard journal 78
accounting year
  closing 98
allowed posting dates
  restricting 101
analysis views
  about 125
  as source of account schedules 128
  by dimension 127, 128
  creating 126, 127
  using 127
audit report 38

B

bank account currency restrictions 71
bank account posting groups 146
bank account reconciliation
  creating 72
bank data conversion service
  about 64
  used, for making payments 65, 66, 68

budget fixed asset transactions 177
budget, for future acquisition costs
  demonstrating 178
budgets
  about 133
  creating 134
  using 138
Business Intelligence (BI)
  using, in Microsoft Excel 130, 131
  using, in PowerPivot 130, 131

C

cancel FA entries 93
cash flow management
  manual expenses 141
  revenues, creating 141
  setup 142
  sources 138
charts
  adding, to Role Center page 122
  displaying 121
  show as chart option 122
checks
  creating 54
Close Income Statement batch process
  running 99, 100
Consolidated Trial Balance 106
consolidation
  performing 103
  performing, on single database 103, 104
  performing, with different database 104, 105
  performing, with other application 106
costing methods, inventory valuation
  average 94
  First In First Out (FIFO) 94
  Last In First Out (LIFO) 94
  specific 94

standard 94
credit cards
  using 51, 52
CRONUS Canada Inc. 27
currencies 155
customer balances
  about 55
  paid invoice, checking 56
  vendor balances 57
customer card
  balance 14
  entries 14
  history 14
  opening 13, 14
  statistics 14
customer ledger entries 28
customer posting groups 146

D

Data Exchange Framework 70
deferrals
  about 109
  using 110, 111
depreciation
  automatic depreciation 172
  calculating 171
  calculating, automatically 173
  manual depreciation 171
  posting 171
dimensions
  about 113
  global dimensions 114
  rest of the dimensions 114
  setting up 150
  shortcut dimensions 114
  using, on documents and journals 115
disposals
  posting, through FA G/L Journal 176
document approval 31
document exchange service 162
document management 162
documents
  about 22
  open documents 29
  posted documents 29

workflow 30
working 23
due dates, managing
  Payment Terms page 39, 42
  about 39
  prepayment processing flow 44
  prepayments 42
Dynamics 365 Business Edition 196
Dynamics 365 Enterprise Edition 196
Dynamics NAV 2016
  functional areas 8
Dynamics NAV
  about 8
  examples 9
  no Save button 11
  posted data cannot be modified scenario 11

E

e-services 162
Electronic Data Interchange (EDI) 9
Enterprise Resource Planning (ERP) 8
eXtensible Business Reporting Language (XBRL)
  162

F

FA G/L Journal
  used, for posting disposal 176
  using, for manual depreciation 172
FA register report 195
filtering expressions
  reference 118
filters
  applying, on pages 116
  using 116
financial consolidation, setting up
  about 106
  business units, defining 107
  chart of accounts, translating 108
Financial Management
  about 8
  significance 10
financial statements
  consolidated company, reporting 106
  consolidating 102
  consolidation, performing 103

Fixed Asset card 168
Fixed Asset details report 194
fixed asset posting groups 146
fixed asset process flow
  depreciation 167
  fixed assets setup 167
  insurance 168
  maintenance 168
  posting transactions 167
  statistics and reports 168
Fixed Asset reports
  about 191
  FA register report 195
  Fixed Asset details report 194
  insurance coverage details report 193
  maintenance details report 192
Fixed Asset Setup page 187
Fixed Asset transaction
  about 169
  journals 170
fixed assets
  about 167
  acquiring 170
  acquisition cost, posting 87, 88, 89
  appreciation 175
  creating 87, 88
  depreciation, calculating 90, 92
  disposals 175
  disposing 93
  entries, canceling 93
  insurance information, setting up 187
  linking, to insurance policy 189
  maintenance costs, recording 186
  maintenance information, setting up 183
  maintenance registration and costs 185
  managing 86
  purchasing 170
  reclassifying 179
  revaluating 90
  selling 93
  track, keeping of service visits 185
  transferring 179
  write-down 175
flowfilters
  applying, on pages 118

  using 116
functional areas, Dynamic NAV 2016
  Financial Management 8
  Human Resources 8
  Job 8
  Manufacturing 8
  Purchase 8
  Resource Planning 8
  Sales and Marketing 8
  Service 8
  Warehouse 8

G

G/L account cards
  about 35
  Consolidation tab 36
  Cost Accounting tab 36
  General tab 36
  Posting tab 36
General Journal
  about 37
  entering in 38
general ledger entries 27
General Ledger Setup page 152, 153
general ledger
  about 10
  inventory valuation, posting 96
general posting groups
  about 145, 147
  general business posting groups 147
  general product posting groups 147
general product posting groups 147

H

Human Resources functional area 8

I

IC chart of accounts 158
IC journals 159
insurance card
  creating 188
insurance coverage details report 193
insurance journal
  used, for linking fixed asset to insurance policy
  190

insurance policy
  assets, attaching to 189
  fixed assets, linking to 189
insurance types
  setting up 188
Intercompany (IC) partners 158
intercompany postings
  about 157
  setting up 158
inventory posting groups 146
inventory posting setup 146
inventory valuation
  about 94
  costing method, selecting 94
  item entry costs, calculating 95
  posting, to general ledger 96
  report, running 97, 98
invoice
  Charge (Item) 25
  creating 25
  fixed asset 25
  G/L accounts 25
  Item 25
  Resource 25
item card
  opening 15
item entry costs, calculating
  inbound entries 95
  outbound entries 95
item ledger entries 28
item prepayments 44

J

Job functional area
  about 8
  accounting implications 160
job posting groups 146

L

local currency (LCY) 155

M

maintenance details report 192
manual depreciation
  with FA G/L Journal 172

Manufacturing functional area
  about 8
  accounting implications 161
master data
  about 12
  customer card 12, 14
  default dimensions, defining 114, 115
  item card 15
  locations 17
  resources 17
  vendors 17
Microsoft Dynamics 365 196
Microsoft Excel
  Business Intelligence (BI), using 130, 131

N

NAV
  incoming payments 69
  outgoing payments 69
number series 151

O

open documents 29
Optical Character Recognition (OCR) service 164

P

pages
  filters, applying 116
  flowfilters, applying 118
payment application rules 64
payment methods
  using 51, 52
payment reconciliation
  about 62
  activities, performing 62
payment registration functionality
  about 58
  Change Amount Received or Date Received 59
  finance charge for overdue amounts 61
  Lump Payment 60
  payment discounts, handling 62
  performing 58
payments
  posting 52, 53
posted documents 29

posted invoice
  customer ledger entries 28
  general ledger entries 27
  item ledger entries 28
  resource ledger entries 28
  TAX entries 27
posting groups
  about 27, 145
  general posting groups 145
  specific posting groups 145, 146
  TAX posting groups 145
PowerPivot
  Business Intelligence (BI), using 130, 131
prepayment processing flow
  about 44
  general ledger setup 45
  general posting setup 45
  prepayment percentage, assigning 46
  prepayments, setting up 44
  process 47
  sales & receivables setup: 46
  steps 48, 49, 50
prepayments
  about 42
  customer and vendor prepayments 43
  item prepayments 44
pricing
  about 17
  purchase pricing 22
  sales discounts 20
  sales prices 18
process
  testing, in Sales Invoice 165
Project Maderia 196
Purchase functional area 8
purchase pricing 22

R

recurring journals
  about 37, 78
  allocations 79, 80
  Expiration Date field 79
  Recurring Frequency field 79
  Recurring Method field 79
reports

  using 120, 121
resource ledger entries 28
Resource Planning 8
Reversing Journal 37
Role Center page
  charts, adding 122

S

Sales and Marketing functional area 8
sales discounts
  defining 20
Sales Invoice
  process, testing in 165
sales prices
  defining 18
SEPA credit transfer
  used, for making payments 65, 66, 68
Service functional area 8
  accounting implications 161
Simple Mail Transfer Protocol (SMTP) 165
specific posting groups
  about 145, 146
  bank account posting groups 146
  customer posting groups 146
  fixed asset posting groups 146
  inventory posting group/inventory posting setup
    146
  job posting groups 146
  vendor posting groups 146
standard journal
  about 37, 77
  creating 78
  using 78

T

TAX Calculation Type
  full VAT 149
  no taxable VAT 149
  normal 149
  reverse change 149
  sales tax 149
TAX entries 27
TAX posting groups 145, 149
transactions
  posting, on closed year 102

V

value entries 28
Value-Added Tax (VAT) 81, 82
VAT Business Posting groups 81
VAT Product Posting groups 81
VAT settlements 83, 84
VAT statements
  running 84, 85, 86
vendor payments
  suggesting 54
vendor posting groups 146
views
  creating 119, 120

W

Warehouse 8
Warehouse functional area
  accounting implications 161
Work in Process (WIP) 161
workflow configuration
  in NAV 2016 34
workflow template 33
workflows
  about 31
  creating 34
  setup steps 31, 32, 34
World Partner Conference (WPC) 195

www.ingramcontent.com/pod-product-compliance
Lightning Source LLC
Chambersburg PA
CBHW060554060326
40690CB00017B/3703